"I've been encouraged to dream again! In the past it was dreams that moved us from one stage of life to the next. But when recent circumstances brought change, it was different. I was losing hope that I could ever dream again. Dutch's latest book has changed that. Thanks, Dutch! Right book! Right time!"

—Willard Thiessen, New Day Ministries

"Compelling, life-changing, and life-redirecting! This book will stir your faith—our world and our lives will be powerfully changed when each of us becomes an outlet for the dreams of our Creator."

—Jim Hodges, president, Federation of Ministers and Churches International

"As you go through these pages filled with God's truth, your heart is stirred and moved into a place of acknowledging, accepting, and believing the thoughts, ideas, and desires God has placed within you. Expectancy and hope will arise in your spirit for your God-given dreams to become a reality."

—Dr. Ché Ahn, senior pastor, HROCK Church, Pasadena, California; president, Harvest International Ministry; international chancellor, Wagner Leadership Institute

"Dream. The word evokes one of two responses in our hearts: excitement and anticipation or sadness and resignation. It all depends on whether we are still dreaming or not. Weaving current, relatable stories of dreamers with scriptural examples of biblical dreamers, Dutch offers us a way to rekindle the dream if it has waned, or stoke the flames if it is roaring in our spirits!"

—Jane Hansen Hoyt, president/CEO, Aglow International

"In the hands of a lesser author—and a lesser man of God—the topic of dreams might become so much pious, self-centered mush. Dutch Sheets gives us just what we dared to hope—a book that is biblical and movingly written and stirs in us the dreams of God."

—Stephen Mansfield, *New York Times* bestselling author

"With humility, humor, and a unique glimpse into the Father's heart, Dutch Sheets explores God's passionate quest for those willing to dream His dreams—men and women God will call friends. At this critical hour in history, *Dream* places a destiny-changing revelation into the hands of the church."

—Colonel Douglas Castle

"If I had read *Dream* without knowing who the author was, I would have said it was Dutch Sheets. I believe he is destined to assist the Bride of Christ as she dreams God's dreams."

—John Kilpatrick, founder and senior pastor, Church of His Presence

Books by Dutch Sheets

FROM BETHANY HOUSE PUBLISHERS

Authority in Prayer
Becoming Who You Are
Dream

DREAM

DISCOVERING GOD'S PURPOSE FOR YOUR LIFE

DUTCH SHEETS

BETHANYHOUSE
a division of Baker Publishing Group
Minneapolis, Minnesota

© 2012 by Dutch Sheets

Published by Bethany House Publishers
11400 Hampshire Avenue South
Bloomington, Minnesota 55438
www.bethanyhouse.com

Bethany House Publishers is a division of
Baker Publishing Group, Grand Rapids, Michigan

Printed in the United States of America

ISBN 978-0-7642-1021-1 (international trade paper)

Library of Congress Cataloging-in-Publication Data
Sheets, Dutch.
    Dream : discovering God's purpose for your life / Dutch Sheets.
        p.   cm.
    Summary: "The author presents God as a dreamer and reveals how God has shared
this nature with His people. Through Bible teaching and personal stories, readers are
shown how to recognize and live out God's plan for their lives"—Provided by publisher.
    Includes bibliographical references (p. 155).
    ISBN 978-0-7642-0947-5 (hardcover : alk. paper)
    1. Dreams—Religious aspects—Christianity. 2. God (Christianity)—Will. 3. Reve-
lation. I. Title.
BR115.D74S54 2012
231'.7'4—dc23   2011045025

All emphasis, shown by italics, in Scripture is the author's.

Unless otherwise indicated, Scripture quotations are from the New American Standard Bible®, copyright © 1960, 1962, 1963, 1968, 1971, 1972, 1973, 1975, 1977, 1995 by The Lockman Foundation. Used by permission.

Scripture quotations identified AMP are from the Amplified® Bible, copyright © 1954, 1958, 1962, 1964, 1965, 1987 by The Lockman Foundation. Used by permission.

Scripture quotations identified KJV are from the King James Version of the Bible.

Any Internet addresses (websites, blogs, etc.) and telephone numbers used in this book are provided as a resource. Baker Publishing Group does not vouch for their content for the life of this book, nor do they imply an endorsement by Baker Publishing Group.

Cover design by Lookout Design, Inc.

Cover photograph © Burgess Blevins/Getty Images

12   13   14   15   16   17   18   7   6   5   4   3   2   1

To Ceci:

When you came along, I knew that dreams really could come true. Thanks for being my best friend and biggest fan, my wisest counselor and most trusted confidant. What a gift you are! You're loving, beautiful, smart, and talented—thanks for marrying "down"!

Let's keep dreaming!

Contents

Contents

Contents

Introduction

THE GIFT

You may not be aware of it, but you have a dreaming nature. You inherited this part of your disposition from your Creator. He created us in His image and likeness so our hearts could relate to His and in order that His dreaming heart could find millions of expressions. You were *designed* to dream, and you *must* dream—*both for yourself and for God*. In fact, if you don't dream with Him, He can't experience all of His dreams and you'll never achieve your destiny.

A life without dreams is like a GPS without a satellite. The GPS might operate, but it would lead you nowhere. Likewise, without God-given dreams to guide you, you will travel life's highway searching for a destination you'll never find. Divinely inspired dreams, on the other hand, will guide you to the destiny He intended for you.

Your Designer dreamed dreams for you before you were even born, then skillfully wove them into your DNA as you were created, along with the ability to find and fulfill them. His destiny for you will be the sum of those dreams. The journey of life, then, is meant to be a dream quest; finding what your Maker has dreamed for you brings life's ultimate satisfaction and should be life's ultimate pursuit.

If you don't discover God's dreams, you'll either waste your life running in wrong races and crossing wrong finish lines or, like many people, have no finish line at all. Other individuals stop running altogether, wandering through life as though it were a maze, hoping they will stumble upon the right exit. What a tragedy. Your Creator doesn't intend for life to be such a gamble. You *can* find His plans and dreams for you and pursue them with confidence.

I want to help you through this book. The inspiration for it began four years ago on a personal retreat, as did a new phase of my own dream quest. The Lord used several things to launch me into this new season: prayer, His Word, a song, the right setting, and a movie. Yep, a movie.

The Ultimate Gift is one of my favorite movies. It's the story of Red Stevens, an older and extremely wealthy businessman who knew he was dying and was trying to decide where to leave his fortune. It seemed his children were money-hungry, self-indulgent, and irresponsible, as were his grandchildren.

All but one.

Jason seemed like all the rest, but Red had seen something else in him, buried under the outer layer of pain, laziness, and his party-driven lifestyle. Red knew that under this stained veneer was great strength and noble character. So Red decided to leave his fortune to Jason—if he passed a series of tests, which Red personally presented posthumously by video. These were difficult, time-consuming tests, some of which took weeks. Jason would only learn of the next challenge after finishing the previous one.

At first Jason resisted—the old man's money could go to charity—he wasn't going to play the game. But after much thought he decided to give it a try, just to get the money. What he didn't know was that each challenge was designed not only as a test but as a character builder and teaching tool—Red called them "gifts, a series of gifts."

It is fascinating to watch the transformation in Jason. He learns the value of hard work, loyalty, giving, family, and several more important qualities needed for a successful and responsible life. Toward the end, he sits down to see the video showing him his next assignment. Grandpa, though now gone, knew when making the videos that if at this point in the process they were still being shown to Jason by his wise and discerning business partner, Jason had passed the tests and could be trusted with wealth.

Almost.

When this latter video begins, Red says, "It's time for you to learn to dream, Jason." Like the character in the movie, I was riveted to the television. *What a concept*, I thought, *the test of dreaming*. Jason was given a very large sum of money and told to do anything he wanted with it. And just in case you decide to watch the movie, that's where I'll stop.

The timing of watching this movie was perfect for me. I was in a season of reexamining my life, analyzing the past and wrestling over the future. As part of this process I planned a week alone to think and pray. I had a cabin reserved for the week, but when I arrived, it just didn't feel right. I decided to follow my heart: *This isn't the place.*

I called my wife, Ceci, and asked her to check the Internet for another place, preferably in Estes Park, Colorado. I would start driving in that direction. The place she found was more than perfect. The altar and cross out back reminded me of Moriah, a special place of dreaming mentioned in Scripture. God knew He and I would dream together in this place.

Perhaps you aren't aware of Moriah and its rich biblical history. It is the mountain where Abraham took Isaac to offer him as a sacrifice. God stopped him, of course. He had only wanted to paint a picture of Himself offering His Son on the cross centuries later. Moriah was the actual place where this would occur! There, on that momentous mountain, Abraham and God dreamed together.

Abraham envisioned the day he would have so many descendants they would be a great nation. God dreamed of the day He would recapture His dream of family. But I'm getting way ahead of myself. We'll visit Moriah later in great depth.

Back to the cabin. No, I wasn't kidding about the altar and cross. Behind the cabin, thirty or so yards from the deck, was a well-built rock-and-mortar altar at the base of a rugged but sturdy wooden cross. There was a beautiful stream just off the deck that forked several yards upstream, then came back together a few yards downstream, forming a small island directly behind the cabin. Someone had gotten onto the island and built the altar and cross—just for me.

Hmm, I thought as I stood gazing at it. *There it is, the place where God recaptured His dream. I wonder what He has in mind for me this week?* I would not be disappointed.

As the week progressed, I found myself being drawn into a thoughtful analysis of my life. *What had I accomplished? Which of these accomplishments were truly worth the time and effort? How many would stand the test of eternity?* As painful as some of it was, I was trying to be brutally and utterly honest. *What dreams had I pursued under the banner of "for the Lord," when my heart had deceived me and they had actually been "for me"?* Many dreams passed the test, some failed. It was painful, but it was good.

At one point the Lord steered my mind toward Jacob, a grandson of the great patriarch Abraham. It seemed that Abraham, like Red, had a grandson with great potential buried under layers of carnality, egotism, and selfish ambition. Jacob, like Jason, had to be transformed and then taught how to dream appropriately.

I saw myself.

It was during that holy time with the Lord that He taught me much of what is in this book. He showed me the process Jacob had to walk through until, like Jason, he was given the ultimate gift. And like his grandfather Abraham, he eventually became God's friend and the two of them dreamed together.

Finally, on that life-changing day several years back, the Holy Spirit shifted my focus from my past to the future. As clearly as though He was in the recliner next to me—He was most definitely present—the Lord began speaking to me about dreaming, just as Red did to Jason. "What are your dreams for the future?" He asked, pulling my innermost thoughts from my heart to my conscious mind.

I thought. I journaled. Hopefully, with a little more clarity of heart and a few decades of added perspective, I dreamed with greater depth and less selfish ambition than I had years earlier. Over the past four decades, climbing the ladder of success has gradually been replaced by plumbing the depths of His heart. Accomplishments are now measured more by heaven's approval than by earth's applause, and making a name has given way to making a difference. At least I believe so.

Eventually, the Lord steered the conversation in a direction that caught me off guard. "Now I'd like to dream a little," I heard clearly. "Would you like to hear some of My dreams?" I listened and I wept. God was trusting me with His dreaming heart. That day remains one of the most holy of my life. I built an altar that day. Not made of rocks and mortar—this one was in my heart.

My greatest goal for this book is that you, too, connect with the dreaming heart of God. If I can enlist you in His dream program by connecting you to His dreaming heart, you'll never again be satisfied with the abnormal existence of a nondreamer or the mundane life of an earthbound one. You were created to dream, and doing so in partnership with God is one of His greatest gifts to us.

You'll also witness God's own agonizing yet wonderful dream journey. Seeing His disappointments and how He overcame them will encourage and inspire you; His wisdom as He does so will amaze you. His is the greatest dream story ever told.

I also pray that as you read the following pages you will do some honest self-analysis, just as I did on my retreat. I believe you will see facets of yourself through dreamers like Adam, Abraham, and many others right up to today. I'm confident that as we look at Jacob and the process he went through to become Israel—this was the name of a person before it was a nation—you will see some characteristics of yourself. And I pray that as you see pieces of your heart still controlled by earthly dreams, you will go to the cross, where God recaptures dreams and hearts, the place where relationship with Him is sealed forever.

Untold pleasure and exciting surprises await you on your dream quest. Like Abraham of old, you'll begin the journey by viewing the Lord as your *God*. As time goes by and the relationship matures, you'll ascend to the understanding that He truly is your *Father*. But the crowning point of a successful life—indeed, the apex of the journey—is when your God and Father has become your *Friend*. God wants to dream with friends.

Let's unwrap the gift!

1

The Power of Dreams

Like you, I've had many hopes and dreams over the years, some frivolous and insignificant, others meaningful and substantive. I recall my first baseball glove—a Pete Rose signature edition, by the way!—which actually had supernatural powers of baseball artistry. I promise it made me a better baseball player. Instantly I was the most excited and envied kid on the block. And, of course, the best baseball player.

Then there was my first new bicycle. Not a used bike, mind you, but a brand-new red, three-speed Schwinn Racer. The world was different from that day forward. Every guy in town was jealous of me and my wheels.

My dreams changed over the years as they graduated to jobs, money, a family, a home—the usual list of American dreams. "With your good looks and intelligence," my mother assured me, "it will hardly be a challenge." (I know what you're thinking, but unlike most moms, mine was very objective.) I went to college to begin my journey toward greatness and was most certainly on my way to success, fame, and fortune . . . that is, until God arranged for me to go on a missionary journey to Guatemala.

What a dirty trick!

I was there when the earthquake in 1976 occurred, killing thirty thousand people in thirty seconds. One million people were left homeless. How do you look into hopeless, grieving eyes and dream of fame and fortune? How do you face a hungry, now fatherless three-year-old and her widowed mother—having to turn them away because you just served the last bowl of soup available in the relief effort—and dream of ease and comfort? My dreams of owning the world transformed into changing it. I've been working at it ever since.

> **Things are supposed to be different on planet earth because you showed up. You're part of the plan.**

You can change the world, too. Things are supposed to be different on planet earth because you showed up. You're part of the plan. A solution, an invention, a prayer, another person yet unborn—there is something in you we need. It begins with a dream.

In his book *A Savior for All Seasons*, William Barker speaks of dreaming. He tells of a disagreement between a traveling bishop and the president of a religious college who also taught physics and chemistry. The itinerant minister persistently contended that we must be near the return of Christ and the beginning of His millennial reign. Why? "Because just about everything concerning nature has been discovered and all inventions created."

The college president disagreed and insisted there would be more discoveries. "Name one," challenged the preacher.

"Well, I'm certain that within fifty years humans will be able to fly," replied the president.

"Nonsense!" shouted the skeptical minister. "Only angels are intended to fly."

The preacher's name? Wright. He had two sons at home, dreamers named Orville and Wilbur—you know them as the innovative Wright Brothers—who proved to have a bit more vision than Dad!

Dreaming ignites creativity. The impossible is powerless against the relentless energy and creative imagination flowing from a dreaming heart. Dreams are pregnant with hope, persistence, ingenuity, and inventiveness—if you dream you will create. Contrarily, if you do not have dreams to pursue, you'll languish and stagnate in a sterile, uninspired, unimaginative, and uninventive world—exactly the way most people live!

Their world is small and confined, restrained by the mundane existence of a nondreamer. For them, the fulfillment of destiny is not accomplished by dreaming, planning, and creativity, but instead is based on chance. God's plan for us, however, is not to spin in circles on the roulette wheel of life hoping we bounce off at the right place and land on success. Our Maker wants us to dream, plan, and create.

Many people are simply waiting for "the big break" or longing to be "discovered"; they trust chance, wandering through life hoping for the right lottery number to appear. Those are fantasies, not dreams. God doesn't want you to live in a fantasy world, waiting for a magical spider bite to launch you on your Spider-Man journey. Just because we're dreamers doesn't mean we have to live in a make-believe world.

The Bible says much about dreaming, and it is enlightening that the concepts of dreaming and creating are both found in the same biblical word. *Yatsar* (Hebrew) means "to create"; *yetser*, a slightly different form of the word, means "imagination, conception, and thought."[1] *Yetser* refers to the plans and purposes formed in the mind, which, of course, include dreaming; *yatsar* is the resulting act of creation. *So the power to create begins with the ability to dream.*

This is exactly how God functions. Isaiah 46:10 states that He declares the end from the beginning. In other words, He sees or imagines the end result (*yetser*), backs up to form the plan or design, then begins creating (*yatsar*). He dreams, then He creates.

Likewise, when God fashioned humans in His image, He placed within us a portion of His ability to imagine and create. We have a God-given ability to conceive something in our mind or heart, which then awakens the creativity and innovation He placed in each of us. Like Him we dream, and then we create the dream. Consider these cases in point.

- We have airplanes because a couple of brothers dreamed we could conquer gravity and fly. Eventually, we went to the moon because someone dared dream we could conquer space.
- We have lightbulbs because a man dreamed of light without a fire. People continued to dream and now we have lasers.
- Telephones were invented because some dreaming mind conceived the outlandish concept of talking through wires. But dreaming begets dreaming, so someone imagined telephones *without the wires* and cell phones were born. Crazy!
- Cars exist because someone dared to dream of a horseless carriage. Henry Ford dreamed of mass-producing these man-made beasts. Another dreamer dreamed of making money by paving roads for those amazing new machines, and, eventually, someone dared to dream of a network of roads all across America *without one single stoplight or stop sign*. Think about it: Through the innovative minds of a few inspired dreamers, traveling went from horse-drawn, covered wagons on rutted, unmapped trails to air-conditioned automobiles on interstate highways (using a GPS, by the way).
- Some nerd dreamed of the computer. Someone "nerdier" dreamed they could be portable—not bad since initially one computer filled up an entire room. Then came the Internet . . . wireless . . . Facebook . . . Twitter . . . Google. And the multizillionaire nerds are still laughing. And tweeting. (Someone even had to dream up new words for all these crazy ideas.)

- Someone dreamed of a television and—it was inevitable—some guy dreamed of changing the channel without getting out of the recliner. Yep, along came the remote. (Sorry, ladies.)

All of these once unbelievable concepts began with a dream. Dreaming, then, unlocked creativity. And by the way, dreams don't have to be big to be substantial in their impact. Consider these "insignificant" dreams:

- Someone got tired of their papers being displaced and dreamed of a paper clip. (They also made sure they were small enough to lose easily so we would have to buy trillions of them.)
- Annoyance over trapped food inspired the toothpick dream.
- A would-be writer grew tired of drawing in the dirt and dreamed of a pencil.
- A guy with sore feet from going barefoot dreamed of sandals. A woman dreamed of making them stylish. Some teenager dreamed of making them comfortable and *voilà*—flip-flops were born! (Go ahead, smile.)

Necessity isn't the mother of invention, dreams are!

Dreams happen! But they don't *just* happen. They're accomplished because dreaming unlocks creativity, innovation, action, and originality. If you don't dream you won't create. Period. End of story. But if you do dream, you *must* create. Necessity isn't the mother of invention, dreams are!

Thirteen-year-old Markita Andrews had a dream of taking her mother on a trip around the world. Her father left home when she was eight, and though struggling to make ends meet, it was Markita's and her mother's dream to travel the globe. So when Markita learned that the Girl Scout who sold the most cookies would win an all-expenses-paid trip for two around the world, she decided she would sell the most.

And did she ever.

Markita sold 3,526 boxes of Girl Scout cookies that year and went on to sell 42,000 more boxes. While other Girl Scouts were accepting an assignment, Markita was fulfilling a dream. They sold cookies, she sold a world tour. Her dream led to creativity, which produced a plan: how to dress, the best times to approach people, the most effective way to ask them to buy, and how to overcome rejection. "Don't ask them to buy your cookies," her aunt advised. "Ask them to invest."

"Hi. I have a dream," Markita would say. "I'm earning a trip around the world for my mom and myself by merchandizing Girl Scout cookies. Would you like to invest in one or two dozen boxes of cookies?" It worked.

Actually, it worked more than Markita ever imagined. Dreams have a way of multiplying. Since then she has spoken at sales conventions all over the country, starred in a Disney movie about herself, and coauthored a bestselling book, *How to Sell More Cookies, Condos, Cadillacs, Computers . . . and Everything Else.*[2] Her plan, coupled with hard work, created the fulfillment of her dream.

What an inspiring story. And like Markita, there's a story in you. Yours will be different, but you have one. Yours may not result in a movie and you may not invent something as monumental as the airplane. Nonetheless, you have an important story, written by the very Author of dreaming Himself. The best place to begin your journey is to see what He had in mind when He started this dreaming thing.

For Review

1. Explain the biblical connection between dreaming and creating.

2. Describe a time when an idea, however fleeting, captured your imagination.

3. What was your response to the inspiration? Did your idea move from *yetser* to *yatsar*?

4. How does Isaiah 46:10 relate to dreaming?

5. Have you given value to what seem like small ideas? If not, how can you do so?

6. Decide now to spend a set amount of time every week dreaming and journaling.

2

The Dreaming God

God is a dreamer. His book, the Bible, is actually the story of His dreams. That may surprise you, but it's absolutely true. Some think the Bible is a legalistic rule book or, at best, a boring history book, but nothing could be further from the truth. It's a dream book. Obviously, it contains many precepts and principles, but they are given to us as a road map for life, not a rule book. In Scripture, God shares His dreams with us—in a most vulnerable way, I might add—and invites us to enter His dreaming world. He and His kids were to be the ultimate "dream team."

The dictionary defines a dream as

- a cherished desire
- what is seen, envisioned, or longed for in the mind concerning the future
- unrealized desires, longings, or plans

In light of these definitions, it is obvious that creation's story is that of a dreamer, the tale of a "cherished, unrealized desire" in the heart of God—a longing for family. He who had innumerable angels serving Him had not yet dared to create a being in His own image and likeness. His heart, however, wasn't satisfied having only angels with which to relate. Certainly these amazing creatures were a wonderful part of His company, and I'm sure they brought Him pleasure, but they weren't family.

God desired sons and daughters; He also longed to have a suitable companion for His Son. To accomplish this He would create the human race in His own image and likeness, far different from the angels. He would even give this new "species" the amazing ability to procreate other eternal spirits. That fact is almost dumbfounding.

For five days the Creator worked on their "home." In Genesis we read of His meticulous creation of the heavens and earth, the sun and moon, animals and plants. He separated night from day and established the boundaries of the seas and land.

Angels must have watched with great fascination as various plants, seeds, mountains, rivers, and oceans were formed. I can't imagine they were surprised at the power of His words or the creative force of the Spirit's hovering. Having always lived with God, they were aware of His greatness. However, they were probably curious throughout the week and perhaps even found some of the creatures humorous. Was there laughter at the elephant's trunk or the zebra's stripes? Did they "ooh" and "ah" at the beauty of the butterfly or majesty of the eagle, the speed of the cheetah or might of the lion?

We're not given the answer, though I suspect this was the case. Job seems to imply that the angels sang and shouted for joy during creation (see Job 38:7). It's not difficult to imagine high praise erupting from them as mountains sprang up, waves began rolling, birds started singing, and flowers commenced their blooming.

Then came day six, the day humans were formed. My guess is the atmosphere changed, angelic mouths hung open in silence, and eyes stared in wonder as the Creator stopped speaking and with His own hands began to shape . . . *What was this to be? Indeed, it must be special if He needs to form and mold it with such meticulous attention,* they may have thought. *Look at the care with which He is forming and handling this creature.*

But wonder became shock and awe as He brought this still lifeless creature—which had an uncanny resemblance to the Creator Himself—into an embrace and what looked like a kiss! God breathed out, Adam breathed in, and emerging from a hidden place in His dreaming heart a created being described as "a little lower than God" stepped into the story (see Psalm 8:5). This was more than unbelievable; it was unimaginable. God had practically cloned Himself, forming someone in His own image and likeness.

Gene Edwards, with great poignancy and imagination, captures the significance of this amazing moment.

He paused, reached down and scooped up a small handful of earth. He stared at the soil for a moment, then spoke again.

"From this red dirt I will create the highest form of life within the realm of things visible. The creature I am about to bring forth will rule over the material universe just as I rule over the spiritual universe."

With those words spoken, the Lord God began to shape, mold, and model the red dirt.

The angels . . . stared, enthralled at their Lord's intensity. They noted how deeply the aloneness, so uniquely his, was etched upon his face.

Suddenly, the look on the face of the Creator changed. He was searching for something . . . something in his own being. Slowly he drew that element from out of himself and engraved it upon the clay.

With the last sculpting stroke, he stepped back from the moist sod, allowing the angels to have a full view of his completed work. They gasped in amazement and cried together, His image! Visible![1]

It is difficult to imagine what the angels must have felt. God had made an image and likeness of Himself, shaping it with His own hands, then filling it with His very Spirit. His dream of family was coming true. And He was pleased—very pleased. Six times in creation's story our Maker said the progress was "good." I find that fascinating. Was God bragging, patting Himself on the back for a job well done? Of course not—there is no pride in Him. Was He surprised?—"Wow, this is turning out really well!" Certainly that wasn't the case either. A likely explanation is that God was simply voicing the satisfaction of His dreaming heart.

His pleasure increased to its highest level, however, after creating Adam. In the sixth pronouncement that creation was good, the Architect added a word: "This is *very* good." That one word practically leaps off the page at me. Can't you hear the heart of a satisfied dreamer in each of these statements, especially this last one? His plan was coming together, and like a proud parent standing over a newborn baby, Papa God was savoring the moment.

I remember well the birth of our two daughters, Sarah and Hannah. The excitement, contentment, and overwhelming joy I felt when holding them for the first time is hard to put into words, but I can assure you it was *very* good. Jeanette Lisefski, mother of three and founder of the National Association of At-Home Mothers, describes the feeling this way:

> She slips into this world, and into my arms, placed there by heaven. She is straight from God. An indescribable gift. As I look upon her, peace and purity fill the air around her. Through joyful tears I whisper in her ear, "We are glad you are here. We waited so long to see you." She opens her eyes, and I am transformed—a timeless moment filled with the infinity of what life is. In her eyes I see total recognition, unconditional love and complete trust. I am a mother.
>
> Lying on the bed, she sleeps between her daddy and me. We count the toes and fingers and marvel at the perfection in such a tiny form. We look for ways she looks like us, and ways she is uniquely herself. We have nothing to say, but our hearts and minds are full of thoughts—of our hopes and dreams for her, of who she might be, of what gifts she brings with her and how she might touch the world.[2]

If we humans experience such a mix of elation, contentment, and joyful expectation at the birth of our children, what must the Father of all creation and giver of life have felt? One can only imagine.

Following this extraordinary launch of His dream, God further explained His plan, entrusting humans with the stewardship of their amazing home. "You're going to manage earth for us," He said to Adam and Eve (see Genesis 1:26–28). In describing this role, He used Hebrew words that held the meaning of "ruling," "managing," and "governing." He was clearly saying, "Taking care of the planet is now a partnership, a family-run operation. I will dialogue with you, teaching you My ways and communicating with you as My family and friends. You will do the hands-on work of managing this paradise."

That we inherited God's dreaming nature is undeniable.

But there was more. Unlike animals, Adam and Eve weren't programmed to act without thinking; nor would they function like angels, simply waiting for a command and then obeying it. They were processors, thinkers, reasoners . . . and, like their Creator and Father, they would also be dreamers.

"You will also dream with Me, Adam," our Father may have said to him, for it was unquestionably true. "I will reveal to you the laws, secrets, and resources hidden within the earth, and you will use your incredible imagination and intelligence to create with them. You'll discover the laws of physics and harness the powers therein. Your dreaming will be breathtakingly exciting and the results astounding as you think of creative ways to use the resources of your elaborate home. Each new discovery will lead to others and be fascinating beyond your wildest dreams." (Pun intended!)

What a plan.

That we inherited God's dreaming nature is undeniable. And thousands of years and billions of people later, He is still inviting us into His dreaming world—one dreamer at a time.

I realize that religion—a system of works-oriented, structure-based activities through which humankind attempts to find God—makes Him seem cold and distant. But the Bible makes clear that He is the essence and personification of love (see 1 John 4:8). Even after we became separated from Him through Adam's sin, He loved us so much He sent His only Son, incarnated as a human being, to reverse that separation (see John 3:16). The dreaming God was determined that nothing would end His dream of family.

As a result, we can now step back into His dream program. This book is an attempt to enlist you. You were *made* to dream and you *must* dream—both for yourself *and for God*. God is the Author of your dreams, but you're an outlet for His.

There is one more word associated with creation that I find fascinating. The Scriptures tell us that when the Creator had finished launching His dream, He "rested" (Genesis 2:2). For years, this seemed strange to me. I simply couldn't imagine an eternal, all-powerful God needing rest. I remember as a kid trying to imagine Him taking a nap. Of course, God doesn't really sleep. Isaiah 40:28 says He "does not become weary or tired." Some clarification came when I discovered that *shabath*, the word for rest, means simply "to stop or cease from labor or work."

Greater understanding was provided, however, when I discovered that still another definition for *shabath* is "to celebrate." In much the same way that we celebrate certain days, holidays for example, by resting from work, this is a concept of *shabath*. On the seventh day, God stopped working and celebrated! He was so excited about the inauguration of His dream that He decided it would be commemorated with a "rest and celebration day." That puts a new twist on taking a Sabbath! Every seventh day we should all rest and celebrate our membership in God's family.

And so, with creation accomplished, God was now ready to give wings to His dream. One can only imagine what incredible pleasure and joy awaited Him and His family . . . had a horrible interruption not occurred.

And yet, even for this, He had a plan.

For Review

1. Define the concept of a dream in your own words.

2. God is a dreamer. How does creation picture this?

3. What is the significance of God creating us in His own image and likeness?

4. Describe some of the differences between humans and angels.

5. What does it mean to celebrate the Sabbath?

3

The Song

One of the great dream stories of our day bears a striking resemblance to part of God's dream journey. In it can be seen the amazing determination God has of keeping His dream alive and of keeping us in His dream program.

As a contestant on *Britain's Got Talent*, Susan Boyle pursued her lifelong dream of a successful singing career. At forty-seven, her age, plain looks, and shyness caused the judges and those watching to initially be condescending and dismissive of her. Perhaps you saw later how her introduction and opening interview was met with mock smiles and derisive nods by the panel of judges. A few chuckles even arose from the crowd as this misguided dreamer shared her dream.

Then Susan began to sing.

Mouths flew open, applause exploded, and a star—or should I say a dream—was born.

On the surface, the title of her flagship song, "I Dreamed a Dream," taken from the musical *Les Misérables*, seemed perfect for the dream-come-true story of this middle-aged "phenom." The irony, however, is that the song is really quite depressing. It is the story of a person who has completely given up on dreaming and ends with the line, "Now life has killed the dream I dreamed."

What a disheartening statement. How tragic and sad . . . and how oft repeated. But the story didn't end there for Susan Boyle—she robbed the song of its meaning! This amazing lady defied all odds and rode one of the world's most famous "dead dream" songs to her own dream. Incredible. A song about the loss of a dream has now brought inspiration to millions.

A dirge birthed a dream.

God sang one of those songs. His dream had barely begun when the Father of Lies, the dream-stealer, misrepresented His heart to Adam and Eve. "God's holding out on you," was Satan's accusation. "You should come out from under His controlling oppression so you can really dream some big dreams."

What a perversion of truth!

God had already invited Adam and Eve into the most amazing dream partnership ever. He had just created time for them (there's a brain teaser), had fashioned the earth and its incredible bounty for them to steward and enjoy, and had begun the process of relating to them as His family, friends, and co-dreamers. Paradise and unimaginable bliss awaited these first two humans and their eventual family.

Tragedy struck, however, when Adam and Eve bought into Satan's dream-stealing lie. Immeasurable pain ensued and God's dream became a nightmare. Life had tried to kill His dream. It looked as though the Creator's dream was dead before it had yet fully begun. From all appearances, the dream-stealer had won.

But God is an incurable dreamer and refused to give up on His dream! He had, in fact, already planned for this potential setback and was ready with an audacious and incredible plan for the redemption of the dream. It was brilliant, spellbinding, and though successful, very painful.

When God sent His Son to rescue the dream, Christ stepped onto the stage of life and began singing. And what amazing songs He sang. Songs of love, peace, and healing rolled off His lips and out from His hands. Lepers were cleansed and rotting skin was replaced by healthy tissue. Sightless eyes were filled with wonder as they saw the world around them for the first time. Outcast prostitutes felt clean and pure again, paralytics walked, and dead people lived again.

But suddenly, like the high-pitched screech on a beginner's violin, a horrible sound was heard. Love's music stopped and hate's song began. Redemption's song was replaced with a dirge, much like the song Susan Boyle sang.

God was ready with an audacious and incredible plan.

What horrible lyrics were heard as the Author of life and Giver of hope was beaten and tortured. Satan was the songwriter and it seemed that hell itself became the orchestra. In the person of His Son, God's very own blood and mangled flesh—along with history's ultimate injustice—was paraded before His taunting abusers. Mocking laughter and derisive jeers from Satan's kingdom celebrated the apparent final death of God's dream.

But for the Prince of Darkness something began to go horribly wrong. The Son of God persevered in singing death's dirge, and as He did, the hideous lyrics began to be overpowered by His power and purity. In heaven's gallery, a glimmer of hope began to emerge. Could it really be? Yes, the impossible was happening! Through Jesus' shed blood, death was losing its sting, the grave its victory, the destroyer his hold on humanity.

The dirge was birthing a dream!

In the greatest turning of the tables in human history, God was stripping the dream-stealer of his power *and using his own song to do it*! Death lost, life won! When Christ shouted, "It is finished," the music changed, death's song died, and dream's song was reborn. Not only God's, but ours.

I have placed this chapter here, very early in the book, because I know many of you have seemingly had your dreams stolen by life. I want you to keep reading. I want you to dream again. I want you to know that God Himself had His dream stolen but refused to give up. And just as He recaptured His dream, He knows how to turn your dirge into a dream song.

We will revisit this ability of His to resurrect dreams in the next chapter with a testimony of my own recovery from "dying dreams syndrome." But first, consider the following picture.

At the Royal Palace of Tehran, in Iran, you can see one of the most beautiful mosaics in the world. The ceilings and walls flash like diamonds in multifaceted reflections. But to create this priceless work the architect had to rob destruction of its power.

Originally, when the palace was designed, the architect specified huge sheets of mirrors on the walls. When the first shipment arrived from Paris, they found to their horror that the mirrors were shattered. The contractor threw them in the trash and brought the sad news to the architect. Amazingly, he ordered all of the broken pieces collected, then smashed them into tiny pieces and glued them to the walls where they became a mosaic of silvery, shimmering, mirrored bits of glass.[1]

The Architect of life has designed some wonderful dreams for you.

The Architect of life has designed some wonderful dreams for you. If you've been broken, through that brokenness He wants to create a mosaic of His glory and present you to the world as a testimony of His grace and love. Joseph kept dreaming in his prison and ultimately reflected the mosaic of kingly wisdom and godly virtue (see Genesis 38–50). King David kept dreaming, even as an outcast living in the caves of Adullam, and eventually revealed what a man after God's heart looked like (see 1 Samuel 18–31).

God has plans and designs for you, as well. For some they'll be new dreams; for others, they will be broken dreams reconstructed by the Master Dreamer Himself as He transforms your dirge into an anthem. Allow Him to reconstruct, restore, or even recreate His dream inside of you so you can, once again, sing His song and reflect His glory.

You were born to dream.

For Review

1. Explain the irony of Susan Boyle's hit song "I Dreamed a Dream."

2. Can you think of someone who recaptured the power of dreaming? What characteristics have you seen in them that you can learn from?

3. How did Satan, the dream-stealer, interrupt God's dream?

4. Think of a dream you've allowed to die. Is it possible God would want to resurrect it, even if in another form?

5. Think about God's persistence in recovering His dream. Allow this to bring inspiration to you. In what area of life do you currently need to persevere?

4

Born to Dream

H ey, Mom," shouted Sarah, my oldest daughter, "close your eyes until we tell you to open them." Sarah and Hannah were five and three years old at the time—going on twenty and eighteen. The girls were in another room, not yet visible, waiting to make their grand entrance. "Okay, Mommy, open your eyes," cried Hannah.

Into the kitchen paraded two young ladies in Mom's high heels, dresses, purses, lipstick, makeup, and jewelry, ready to strut their stuff. Too pleased and proud to be upset—and hoping the lipstick was smeared only around their mouths and not on the carpet—Mom played along and out came the camera. The Sheets Family Fashion Show was in full swing.

What mother of little girls hasn't experienced something similar? And what parent of little boys hasn't seen them playacting some aspect of being a man—soldiering, hunting, being a sports hero, or going to work? During the years my brother, Tim, and I were growing up, our dad was an evangelist and pastor. Mom has a picture of us at

39

four and three years of age using a small stepladder as a pulpit with a Bible resting on top. We two young boys were fervently "preaching the gospel." Thousands were saved!

Whether it's a small child dreaming of being an adult, a teenager fantasizing about changing the world, or an adult planning their future, we're dreamers all. Some internal force compels us to think about the future: tonight's party, the trip next week, or the expansion next year. Regardless of the theme, we're always thinking about our tomorrows.

We can't help it. It's our nature to dream. Our Creator is a dreamer, and He placed within us His dreaming nature. Made in His image and likeness, we can't simply function like angels or animals, which do not dream. Angels do as they're told and animals act based on instinct or mimic their parents. Even those animals that seem to think ahead—hoarding food for a winter season, building a "home," or flying south for the winter—aren't planning, they're "instincting." On the other hand, when we do these sorts of things, we are planning, imagining, and envisioning the future. We're dreaming.

> **Some internal force compels us to think about the future.**

Unlike my girls fantasizing of being like Mommy, a baby peacock doesn't put on pretend feathers and strut its stuff. A caterpillar doesn't dream of one day having beautiful butterfly wings and colors; it doesn't even wish it could fly. Lions don't invent new ways to kill prey and salmon don't long for the day they swim "home." None of these creatures are blessed and trusted with a dreaming nature. Only humans.

This means the animal world has strict preset limitations as to what they can do and become. Not us. Through the power of imagination and creativity, God has gifted humans with almost unlimited ability and potential. We manage and steward our home—the earth—and its resources. We grow and maximize our inherent gifts and talents, shaping and molding our futures. We build and invent by discovering, harnessing, and utilizing laws of physics and science. We mass-produce materials and reshape earth's elements into steel, concrete, rubber, and other usable products.

Like a thrill-seeking adrenaline junkie, we're hopelessly addicted to the rush of pursuing, discovering, or creating something new. We can't help it. We're made in God's image, therefore we *dream*; we dream, therefore we *create*. The Scriptures actually connect dreaming and creating, a fact I mentioned earlier and will look at more closely later. Observation and history both teach us this is true. If you didn't dream you wouldn't create, for *creating is simply transferring dreams from the realm of thought to the world of reality.*

The story is told about a young misfit nicknamed Sparky who dreamed. And he created. Many obstacles tried to stop him, but the dream survived.

For Sparky school was all but impossible. He failed every subject in the eighth grade. In high school he flunked physics, Latin, algebra, and English. He didn't do well at sports either. He did manage to make the school's golf team but promptly lost the only important match of the season.

Sparky was socially awkward. He was astonished if a classmate ever said hello. And dating? Well, that was totally out of the question. Sparky was a loser and everyone knew it. Somehow he learned to roll with it, learning to be content.

But drawing was important to Sparky, and he was proud of his artwork. Here, too, he would suffer rejection as his drawing submissions would be turned down by Disney and even his school yearbook. More losses for the loser.

Sparky decided to write his own story—a story told by cartoons. He described himself, a little boy who was a loser and a chronic underachiever. And that little boy in the cartoon, who was rejected again and again, is known worldwide as Charlie Brown. The *Peanuts* comic strip helped Charles Schulz go from misfit to sensation.[1]

How fortunate for Charles Schulz, and for cartoon lovers everywhere, that he kept on dreaming. Had he not, the creative wit and imagination in him would have stayed locked up in his brilliant mind. His dream would have never materialized and his destiny would have been lost had he quit.

The dreaming nature in you wants and needs an outlet. If you are not dreaming, a part of who you were made to be has ceased to function. And, as we shall see, if you're not dreaming, you have cut yourself off from at least some portion of your future. *Your destiny needs for you to dream!*

Monty Roberts was the son of an itinerant horse trainer who worked hard training horses at many farms, stables, and ranches. His high school career was continually interrupted because of this work schedule. As a senior, he was asked to write a paper about what he wanted to be and do when he grew up. Monty wrote a lengthy paper describing his goal of someday owning a magnificent horse ranch. He drew a diagram of the two-hundred-acre dream ranch, detailing the location of the buildings, stables, track, and four-thousand-square-foot house. A great deal of his heart went into this project.

A few days later Monty received the paper back from his teacher with a large red F. Upon being asked the reason for the F, the teacher responded, "This is an unrealistic dream for a boy like you. You have no resources or money. You have to buy the land, breeding stock, and pay stud fees, among other things. There's no way you could ever do it." The teacher then added, "If you will rewrite this paper with a more realistic goal, I will reconsider your grade."

Monty thought about it long and hard for a week. Finally, he turned in the same paper, making no changes at all, and informed his dream-stealing teacher, "You can keep the F, and I'll keep my dream."

Years later, Monty's dream became a reality. He now lives on a two-hundred-acre ranch . . . and has his high school paper framed over the fireplace.[2]

Don't allow anything to steal your dream, and don't shut down your dreaming nature. Your destiny is at stake.

A while back I went through a season of hope deferred that tried to force me to stop dreaming. Several important endeavors of our ministry, all connected to my hopes and dreams of seeing a Third Great Awakening in America, were suffering severe setbacks. I grieved deeply because I love this nation so greatly. Simultaneously, I experienced significant betrayal and broken promises, which resulted in the finances of our ministry being seriously impacted. We were nearly broke. Hope deferred began to set in.

> **Don't allow anything to steal your dream. Your destiny is at stake.**

Mentioned in Proverbs 13:12, "hope deferred" is simply a phrase that describes the fruit of broken dreams or failed plans. It happens to everyone—hope deferred is the common cold of the soul. But if not checked, this verse goes on to tell us that it can cause spiritual and emotional heart disease. The result? We stop dreaming and start dying. And, most assuredly, we stop creating.

While I was in this season, I realized that in some areas of my life, I had subconsciously begun to shut down. Though the effects were still fairly subtle at first—most people would not have noticed this was happening to me—my emotions were being affected and my passion was starting to wane. As the results intensified, the inevitable decrease in creativity began. Only dreamers create. Nondreamers sustain and eventually stagnate.

The last thing to leave us in this hope-deferred process is risk-taking. I found myself dangerously close to this, thinking dream-destroying thoughts like, *Why not just take it easy the way most folks do and think more about yourself? Quit caring so much about America, Dutch. You're only setting yourself up for more disappointment. Preach messages and write books that make people happy and you money. Don't sound the alarm about America's condition and don't challenge people. Like so many leaders, simply smile and let people believe everything is okay in our nation. Leave well enough alone. Chill. Play it safe. Stop taking risks.*

My arteries were starting to clog.

If this had continued, my days as a change agent would have been over, for as we all know, only risk-takers are change agents. Those who fear risk will always leave well enough alone. That means they're stuck at "well enough." People who live there standardize mediocrity. And those who play it safe will ultimately have to play by someone else's rules, even if those rules are inappropriate and need to change. I have a bumper sticker on my truck that states this so eloquently: "If you ain't the lead dog, the scenery never changes." I want to risk and I want to change the scenery in America. I don't like the rules of increasingly vocal forces who want to de-Christianize America. And I certainly don't like looking at their backsides!

What did I do to reverse this heart disease? The moment I realized it was happening, I spoke to God about it, telling Him I recognized the symptoms of hope deferred. I thanked Him for revealing this to me and then asked Him to heal and awaken my heart so I could dream again.

He was faithful. As is typical, the process took a little while, but the Holy Spirit has reenergized me. That's why I'm writing this book. I'm dreaming again and excited about the future—even its risks.

Ronald Meredith, in his book *Hurryin' Big for Little Reasons*, describes one quiet night in early spring:

Suddenly out of the night came the sound of wild geese flying. I ran to the house and breathlessly announced the excitement I felt. What is to compare with wild geese across the moon?

It might have ended there except for the sight of our tame mallards on the pond. They heard the wild call they had once known. The honking out of the night sent little arrows of prompting deep into their wild yesterdays. Their wings fluttered a feeble response.

The urge to fly—to take their place in the sky for which God made them—was sounding in their feathered breasts, but they never raised from the water.

The matter had been settled long ago. The corn of the barnyard was too satisfying! Now their desire to fly only made them uncomfortable.[3]

If you've stopped flying, determine to start again. If you've stopped dreaming, tell the naysayers they can keep their F; you were made to dream. If loss or pain has created hope deferred in you, ask God to heal your heart and awaken your dreaming nature. He will do so. Job 14:7–9 says, "There is hope for a tree, when it is cut down, that it will sprout again. . . . At the scent of water it will flourish and put forth sprigs like a plant."

There is hope for you, also. Be like this tree. Put your nose to the wind and see if God won't send the sweet fragrance of a dream wafting your way. He will. He loves to give new beginnings, and He loves it when you dream.

For Review

1. What are some practical indicators that it is in our nature to dream?

2. This chapter states, "If you didn't dream you wouldn't create." Explain why this is true.

3. Explain "hope deferred."

4. List the progression of hope deferred and its effect on dreaming.

5. What can be done to awaken dreams again?

5

Destiny Dreaming

When Steve Cauthen was nine, his job was helping his father on the farm. In between pitching hay, he liked jumping on the packed bales, pretending he was on a racehorse. Once when his father said, "Stop daydreaming, boy, and put the bale in the truck," Steve answered, "I will as soon as I win the Belmont Stakes." And sure enough, the young man who was riding a bale of hay did go on to win the Triple Crown at age eighteen. His dream at the age of nine propelled Steve Cauthen to become one of the most successful jockeys in the world.[1]

You gotta love it!

Dreams and destiny are connected. If you don't dream you'll never achieve your destiny. A desire to discover and fulfill one's purpose is one of the strongest forces driving us. But do we really have a God-given purpose? We all want one, at least that's what the surveys show.

USA Today did a poll a few years ago. In this survey they asked randomly chosen individuals what one question they would most like to ask God. I expected the most-asked question to concern the eternal fate of a deceased loved one, or perhaps why suffering exists, maybe even where the individual being interviewed would spend eternity. Nope. First place went to—you guessed it—the purpose-seekers, who asked, "What is the purpose of my existence?" Twice as many polled asked this question than any other.

I was shocked. People, as a whole, care more about significance than where they'll spend eternity.

This has become the number one concern raised by college students in America to their counselors and professors. They want more than a career; they want to believe their lives make a difference for others.

I suppose I shouldn't have been surprised. I have long been aware of the innate craving every person has for a sense of worth and value. These facets of a healthy self-image are connected to our belief that our life does indeed have purpose. Perhaps Myles Monroe had it right when he said, "The greatest tragedy of life is not death but life that fails to fulfill its purpose."[2]

The dictionary defines *purpose* as "an anticipated outcome that is intended or that guides your planned actions" and "the reason for which something is done or created or for which something exists." Expanding purpose to the concept of destiny brings a Creator into the picture; it is the belief that *He* mandated our existence, then created us with design and intent.

Psalm 139:13–18 substantiates this belief. The entire passage relates to our topic, but verse 16 is especially poignant: "Your eyes have seen my unformed substance; and in Your book were all written the days that were ordained for me, when as yet there was not one of them." *Ordained* is from the Hebrew word *yatsar*, which, as we mentioned in our opening chapter, is also one of the biblical words for *create*. Since a creator has a purpose in mind for his creation, the word also means "predestined." This passage emphatically states that God determined a destiny for us and recorded it in a book *before we were even born*. (Wouldn't you love to take a look inside that book!)

The New Testament confirms this. The word *purpose* is from the Greek word *prothesis*. The prefix *pro* means "pre" or "beforehand," and you can easily guess the meaning of the root word *thesis*. Our English term thesis—a report or essay explaining a theory, study, or design—is derived from this word. God "prethesis-ed" our lives. This is precisely what Psalm 139:16 so eloquently states.

If this were not reassuring enough, not only did God design a plan, creating a *what* and a *why* for us, He also chose our *when* and *where*. Acts 17:26 says He "determined [our] appointed times, and the boundaries of [our] habitation." You can rest assured that no part of your existence is accidental, not even the time and place of your birth. He knows when your mark is needed on history.

During the late 1700s the Lord chose a remarkable destiny for a young man in England, one that would help to shape the history of a nation. And as Steven Dyer writes, the date of that man's departure to heaven, well, that too would prove to be profoundly significant.

The movie *Amazing Grace* tells the story of William Wilberforce, who led the efforts to eradicate slavery from Great Britain. When asked by his butler after his conversion if he had found God, Wilberforce's reply was, "I think He found me."

Indeed, God found Wilberforce, who became so joined to His heart and desires that ultimately, no price was too great for the dream. His passion to see slavery end was so overwhelming that it resulted in stomach ailments, nightmares, ridicule and four decades of tireless work. But days before his death the decisive vote came to eliminate slavery from England. When the law became formal three days after the vote, Wilberforce's spirit left this world. Thomas Buxton, a member of the House of Commons at the time, said of Wilberforce, "The day which was the termination of his labors was the termination of his life."[3]

What an example of God choosing our times and seasons. Most of us will never be as famous as Wilberforce, but that shouldn't be the goal of our dreaming. Our striving should be to find recognition in heaven, not on earth. God has need of you just as He did Wilberforce. Since God never acts without purpose, the fact that you're alive is proof that you have something this generation needs.

Being confident we have a destiny, however, isn't enough. Like Steve Cauthen riding his bale of hay or something weightier like Wilberforce hoping to see the injustice of slavery terminated, your God-given destiny is inextricably connected to dreaming. Like Batman and Robin, crime fighters extraordinaire, these two elements involving your future are joined at the hip, two peas in a pod, birds of a feather—okay, I'll stop with the clichés, but make sure you get it: They are connected. One can't function without the other. *We're destined to dream and we dream for our destiny.*

> **As we seek God's will for our lives, He places desires in our hearts.**

Think of dreams as your destiny broken up into stages. Your life won't consist of one dream, but many. All of us will have different dreams for the various areas of our lives—work, family, pleasures, and so on—and also for each season. If we allow our Creator to influence this process, He will direct us toward our purpose and destiny *from dream to dream.* As we seek His will for our lives, He places desires in our hearts, knowing that when fulfilled, they will prepare us for (and many times lead us to) the next stage. *Life, then, should be a series of dreams which, when added together, equal our destiny.* Like a diorama, which is a picture or series of pictures representing a continuous scene, this is our "dreamorama."

If you do not dream, your life will become too random, driven by the winds of circumstances or the fickleness of your emotions. Spontaneity is wonderful, but your purpose and destiny require the deliberateness of dreaming. If at one time you dreamed but have ceased doing so, your destiny has stalled.

Everything I've done in my ministry has been built on activities of the past. Years ago I dreamed of being an effective and powerful intercessor, which then led to thousands of hours of reading and study. That led, fifteen years later, to writing a bestselling book on intercession, *Intercessory Prayer*. Youth pastoring, missions, worship leading, teaching in a Bible institute, being a senior pastor—all of those destiny stages have been used by God to fashion my dreamorama.

I am obviously not referring to insignificant dreams such as going to a Super Bowl or jumping from an airplane—the average "bucket list"—unless of course you're dreaming of being a football player or a paratrooper. These fun goals are good and add spice to life, giving us something to look forward to, but they aren't destiny dreams. What I'm referencing are life-directing goals on the level of finding one's spouse, raising children, choosing and pursuing a career, and what we do throughout life to serve God and others. These important decisions connect with one another to form our dreamorama and fulfill our destiny.

On occasion we are surprised at some of the twists and turns, and then we glance backward. We see how God carefully wove us, even placing His desires and dreams in our hearts. We thought they were ours. He knew all along they were His.

Friends of ours experienced this in a most profound way. Read Elizabeth Wilkerson's story, in her own words, and see how she and God dreamed together for a little girl in Africa. It's longer than what would typically be used to illustrate a point, but the entire story is so good I've included it in its fullness. Get some tissues ready and enjoy.

While most young girls my age had New Kids on the Block posters plastered on their walls, bulletin boards in my room reflected a different desire: African orphans. They were all shapes and sizes but with one common denominator: They were African and they had taken my heart. It was not something I could articulate; after all, I had never been to this vast continent nor was I even old enough to be married or have children. Nevertheless, I would dream about

51

my daughter. She was there, I was sure of it. One day I would go to Africa and bring her home.

Throughout my college years I took many missions trips and studied with YWAM. Still my toes had never graced African soil. She remained there, in the back of my heart, and I yearned to know her.

When my husband and I first met, I grilled him regarding his thoughts on adoption and specifically adopting an African child. He was all-in for any sort of adoption or foster care God would call us to. We were married and had our first daughter, but still we waited.

After a painful miscarriage and season of refinement, I was worshiping the Lord and I saw her, in a vision. I had my biological daughter Clara on my left and my African daughter on my right. In one quick breath the Lord had restored hope to me. I went to my husband and shared what I had seen. He said, "I believe this could now be the time to start pursuing adoption."

Over the course of the next few weeks, we received information from over ten adoption agencies. I sat on my bed buried in pamphlets and brochures and wept. Starting and completing an international adoption was beginning to feel like climbing Mount Everest, another pie-in-the-sky dream. The cost? The time? The unknowns?

Perplexed and overwhelmed, we went to church like any other Sunday. We had a guest speaker that day; she regularly attended our church, although I had yet to meet her. She began to speak and my mouth dropped open. She conveyed her heart for Ethiopian orphans and shared about the orphanage she ran there. She informed us about the adoption agency she worked with to place these kids into loving homes.

We chased her down after church and drilled her with all our questions. Within minutes, so many of our initial fears were put to rest, and one week later we turned in our application and started the mountain of paper work.

Our adoption officially started June 2008. There were hurdles to work through—in the beginning, primarily financial. My dream had always included my being older and more established, so we could fund it ourselves. The timing was clearly the Lord's, so my faith was going to have to stretch. Our $1,000 emergency fund was not going to go far in funding a $30,000 adoption. Nevertheless, we plugged along. Whenever we had to write a check, the money was always there, miraculously. We were given funds, we hosted a dinner, my husband received extra work, we received a grant, and we had many garage sales.

On May 27, 2009, we saw her picture for the first time in an email our agency sent to us. We were on our annual family vacation, and receiving this was the last thing I expected. The email was simple, but her picture was not. She captivated us from the moment we first saw her. Her big brown eyes were blank and expressionless, yet they called to me.

> **"The timing was clearly the Lord's, so my faith was going to have to stretch."**

Our biggest hurdle came and lingered—her paper work. There were constant complications, errors, and delays. Her case was extremely unique, and our agency worked around the clock to get her to us. We waited and prayed. After nine months of valiant effort, our agency called. "We don't think we can bring her home. Would you consider another child?" That was out of the question. For nine months we had prayed for her by name. She was as real to me as my daughter sitting next to me. If we didn't contend for her, who would? She would be our daughter, no matter how long it took. So we prayed and fasted.

On my birthday six weeks later, an unexpected knock came to our front door. I walked out to a barrage of balloons and three signs that read "YOU PASSED COURT." My knees went weak and tears exploded from my eyes. She was ours, legally ours. My husband and I stood, shocked. We didn't even know we had a court date. Our adoption director informed us that even she didn't know about our court date. To make it even better, our daughter passed court the same day as her best friend from her orphanage. He was going to a family in our city only three miles away. Their friendship would remain intact.

One month later my husband and I boarded the plane bound for Addis Ababa, Ethiopia. On May 2, 2010, we walked into a dark orphanage room filled with napping toddlers. In the corner, she stood dressed in the dress I had sent months before. I went to her and her big brown eyes stared up at me. She allowed me to hold her and didn't let go all week. There were surprisingly very few tears—just a deep knowing that we belonged together, and had for a very long time. We returned home from Ethiopia on, extraordinarily, Mother's Day, 2010, to a mass of family and friends waiting at the airport to celebrate our daughter Moriah. It was then my tears came. For the first time in her life she was being celebrated. She was home.

Our daughter was a malnourished and downcast orphan. Today she is a chubby-faced, vivacious little girl. I was recently walking through a store with her, and a stranger came up to me and asked, "Why did you adopt?" Then I remembered my bulletin board from years ago, and I smiled and responded, "I have always known I had a daughter in Africa."

She was mine and I was hers. Before I ever knew her she was written on my heart, a part of my destiny.

Heavenly dreams? Most definitely!

Destiny dreams? Just ask Moriah.

Dreaming with God is so much more exciting than dreaming earthbound dreams! Don't miss your destiny by giving your passions only to temporal desires. Ask your Maker to awaken in you the passions He hid in your heart—and wrote in His book. As He does, according to one Old Testament verse, at least six things will occur.

For Review

1. Combine and rewrite the dictionary definitions for *purpose* given in this chapter.

2. How do the Old Testament and New Testament references reinforce this definition and enhance it from God's perspective?

3. Explain the meaning of the Greek word *prothesis*. How does it relate to *yatsar*?

4. Explain what a "dreamorama" is.

5. Share your dreamorama up to this point in time. Note the dreams where you allowed God to influence the process, and those dreams where you did not. Also include fun goals, life goals, and the times when you were not dreaming.

6

Dream or Decorate

No one imagined Charles Dutton would ever amount to anything, for he spent many years imprisoned for manslaughter. When asked how he was able to make such a remarkable transition, this now-successful Broadway star replied, "Unlike the other prisoners, I never decorated my cell."[1]

The mundane art of cell decorating is common but unnatural—it's a learned art. Unintended for us by our Creator, this practice is the equivalent of being dreamless or purposeless. Decorating one's cell means we have resolved ourselves to making a current rut permanent.

You don't have to be in a prison to live in a cell. Your current job could be one; perhaps the job you just lost, having imprisoned you in unpleasant circumstances, is your prison cell. The relationship you lost, the abuse you suffered, the poverty in which you were raised, the injury you incurred, the personal challenge that you seem unable to conquer—cells come in all shapes and sizes. If allowed, they will imprison you in a confined place of isolation, despair, hopelessness, and inactivity. Their ultimate effect, if not checked, will be to rob you of your future.

There is good news, however, concerning this Alcatraz of the soul. You possess a key that will unlock this cell's door. What is this key? Dreaming. The only thing that can keep you locked in your cell is losing the will to dream. You'll have to either dream or decorate.

Proverbs 29:18 speaks of the death sentence that comes from being dreamless: "Where there is no vision, the people perish" (KJV). It doesn't get any plainer than that. If you don't dream, you'll die. Perhaps you won't perish physically, but a part of you certainly will, and it will be the part that makes you truly live life. As William Wallace in the movie *Braveheart* said to the cell-bound men of Scotland, men who were afraid to fight for freedom from the tyranny of Britain, "Every man dies; not every man really lives."

Truer words were never spoken.

Like a hidden, corroding battery inside a flashlight, you can look good on the outside but be dying on the inside. Cell decorating also requires a degree of denial. Hiding behind a well-disguised façade, while actually plagued with the inability to live life to the fullest, is exactly what this verse in Proverbs is describing. The word *perish* is actually more associated with this figurative meaning than it is with physical death.

You can look good on the outside but be dying on the inside.

There was a season of my life several years ago when I felt directionless and imprisoned by my circumstances. I was determined not to decorate my cell but couldn't find the key to the door.

I was working for a church in Oklahoma that Ceci and I believed was moving in the wrong direction, and we also felt that my gifts were not being utilized appropriately and, therefore, not being developed. Being uncertain of what to do, we asked some friends of ours to pray for us, and we, too, went into a season of prayer for direction.

A day or so later, one of these friends called me. "I was praying for you and received a mental picture which I believe was from the Lord," he told me.

I was excited, thinking this could be my answer. "What did you see?"

"There was a circle painted on the ground and you were walking on this circle."

"What else did you see?" I asked excitedly. I was expecting some profound revelation, perhaps similar to the Old Testament prophet Ezekiel's "wheel in the middle of a wheel" vision; or perhaps I was circling the target ready to land.

"That's it," he said. "You were just walking in circles, over and over."

"That's it?"

"Yep. That's all I saw."

At first I was irritated. *How encouraging,* I thought. *My word from the Lord is that I'm going in circles. Thanks a lot!*

The more we prayerfully considered the picture, however, the more we realized it was the simple answer we had been looking for. I was in a dreamless, confused state of mind, while at the same time working in a situation that was leading me nowhere. The solution, one that we hadn't wanted to hear, was that I would have to resign and move on.

It is always appropriate to serve someone else's dream, which I was faithfully doing at the time, but only when the Lord is directing one to do so. When we are doing so at His leading, this will always further equip us for our destiny and steer us in the right direction. If it isn't God's will, however, it will cause setbacks or loss.

I decided to get off of the circle and back on course. I looked inward, reconnected with the dreams God had given Ceci and me, and the Lord was faithful to move us into His plan for us. Had we remained in that situation, portions of our destiny could very possibly have "perished." Don't ever settle for such an outcome. God always has a way to direct you toward life and purpose.

Perish comes from the Hebrew word *para*, and when fully understood it reveals several ways dreamlessness can imprison us. The opposite and positive effect is also true, however, and understanding this term brings wonderful revelation of how vision frees and empowers us. In this and the next chapter, I want to point out six of these important meanings.

First, *para* means *unbridled, uncontrolled,* or *unrestrained.* Where there is no dream or vision, we are like a horse without a bridle or a car without a steering wheel or brakes: out of control and headed for disaster. Activity alone doesn't equal progress, and busyness doesn't equate to productivity. Hard work in and of itself doesn't guarantee success, nor does the admirable character trait of perseverance. Something must direct these efforts and qualities, and that something is a clear vision. Someone once said, "If you don't know where you're going, any road will take you there."

A bridle, providing a connection point for a horse's reins, illustrates this well. It allows the rider of a horse to control its great strength and ability, making these things work for him, not against him. An out-of-control horse is not only unproductive, it is dangerous and destructive. With a bridle and reins, however, a rider can turn a horse with just a gentle tug. It's not difficult to see how dreams function in this way, keeping us moving in the right direction.

Dreams not only steer us, they also provide restraint. Where there is no vision, people are unrestrained. It is easier to refrain from overspending, for example, when one is saving money for a specific cause. Whether it is a child saving her allowance to purchase a bicycle or a married couple saving funds to buy a home, vision produces self-control.

While I was in high school, my dream was to be the starting quarterback on the varsity football team. Not exactly a world-changing ambition, but, nevertheless, it was at the top of my list. I had only begun to play this position as a sophomore and had a lot to learn in order to make this a possibility.

Other players on the squad had more talent, but heart often wins over giftedness, and like a bulldog on a bone, I grabbed hold of my dream and went to work. When practices ended, I would go home and practice some more. While my teammates spent their free time on fun activities and entertainment, my dream brought me discipline and restraint. I studied the quarterback position, threw footballs thousands of times, practiced hand-offs to make-believe players, and even envisioned myself in imaginary games.

The hard work paid off. I matured quickly into a good quarterback, and before my sophomore season was over, I was the starter. Dream realized! It was awesome—Friday night lights, big man on campus, newspaper interviews, and more. It was difficult to remain humble in my greatness, but somehow I managed!

The second meaning of *para* is somewhat unusual; it can actually mean *naked*. The concept is often figurative, referring to one that is *uncovered* or *unprotected*, whether physically, emotionally, or spiritually. The word could actually be translated "exposed." Where there is no vision, people are unprotected and vulnerable to wrong choices, compromise, and distractions that waste time and energy.

For example, a dream of saving oneself sexually for their spouse can protect a young person from sexual compromise; a goal of staying out of debt can ward off frivolous or unwise expenditures; and dreams involving destiny can shield one from pursuing wrong careers and activities.

In 1991, just after moving to Colorado for the purpose of writing and taking a partial sabbatical, I was offered the pastorate of a very large church in Florida. The current pastor and founder of the congregation wanted to retire and was searching for his successor. Though I didn't feel the position was right for me, out of respect for this person I agreed to at least travel there to hear his proposal.

The offer was generous and enticing. The church had just completed a new and beautiful sanctuary, the salary would be much more money than I had ever made, and my young family would be secure for years to come. At one point the pastor actually held the keys of this new building up to me and with tears in his eyes begged me to take them.

I was ready to do some serious decorating!

My dad heard about the offer and, I'm sure picturing me as a starving author in Colorado, pleaded with me to take the offer. Others also advised me to do so.

After much prayer, I said no.

My dream was to write. I also felt called to the entire nation of America, and also to travel and teach on the subject of prayer, something I wouldn't have been able to do while leading a large congregation. It was a huge test, but my dream protected me. We stayed the course and remained in Colorado Springs. It was a short time later that my first book, *Intercessory Prayer*, was written. I also became one of the leaders of the worldwide "prayer movement." *Intercessory Prayer* is now in more than thirty languages and I have authored seventeen other books.

I often wonder what would have happened had I taken that offer. Would I have written books? Would I have connected with the necessary leaders in the prayer revival? Many lived in Colorado Springs. It's impossible to know for certain, but I likely would have missed portions of my dream and destiny.

Some see obstacles, dreamers see possibilities!

Still another concept of *para* has helped decorate more cells than you can imagine. "Perish" means to be *unready* or *unprepared*. Dr. Spiros Zodhiates, in his lexicon, says it is used to describe missing an opportunity by letting it slip through the fingers.[2] Where there is no vision or dream, opportunities will be missed. On the other hand, focused vision produces alertness to opportunity.

A person who dreams of becoming wealthy through real estate will see building and land opportunities others miss. During the Great Depression there were more millionaires created than in any other time in history. While many people decorated their cells, others were dreaming about opportunities. One who dreams of winning souls will see the potential in a sinful individual, whereas someone else may see only their sinfulness. Jesus saw something more than a prostitute in Mary Magdalene; He saw a potential follower and helped her undecorate her cell. He hates decorated cells.

Perhaps you've heard of Ned and Jed. They were seeking their fortune hunting wolves—a $5,000 bounty was being offered for wolves captured alive. Exhausted, they fell asleep one night dreaming of their soon-to-come riches. A few hours later, Ned awoke to see them surrounded by forty wolves with bared teeth. Nudging Jed, he whispered, "Wake up, Jed. We're rich!"

Some see obstacles, dreamers see possibilities!

Ned is my kind of guy; he saw past the adversity to the opportunity. The world around us is filled with both. The problem is that most of us aren't looking for the opportunities; *and we aren't looking because we aren't dreaming.* The busyness of decorating our cells has distracted us, even made us feel productive. This would be a good time to remove and demolish all of the decor—every picture, the figurines, the souvenirs. Get rid of everything that makes you feel comfortable in a dreamless world.

Ask God to awaken your dreaming nature. Expect Him to energize you with creativity and passion. He wants you to live—really live—and fulfill the destiny He planned for you.

It's time to decorate the dream.

For Review

1. Can you think of a time in your life when you "decorated your cell"? What could you have done differently to break out of the circumstance you were in?

2. Think of a situation in which your dream or vision protected you from going in a wrong direction. Write down any

lessons you can now see from this that could help you in the future.

3. *Perish* from Proverbs 29:18 also means to be naked. How does this strange definition relate to vision?

4. Explain how a dream produces alertness to opportunity and vice versa.

5. Do you know anyone with a decorated cell? Ask the Lord if He would have you share some of the thoughts in this chapter with them.

7

Get Motivated

Turning thirteen was the point in life when I decided to declare my freedom from the tyranny of my controlling and unreasonable dad. He mistreated me by requiring me to perform various chores around the house—menial jobs such as lawn mowing, washing the car, taking out the trash, and other things he deemed appropriate.

One day at school my friend Randy informed me that I was being abused. He told me I should be paid for the work I did around the house and that I should go "on strike" for fair wages. I didn't know what going on strike meant, but Randy said it simply meant to stop working until you are paid what you deserve for the work you do.

"Also, how much do you get for an allowance?" he continued as he instructed me on the rules of fair family compensation.

"I don't get an allowance," I said. "I work for my spending money by shining dad's shoes, mowing other people's lawns, and operating a small paper route."

Randy was astonished. He proceeded to explain that I should receive a fair allowance, as well as be paid for the work I perform.

Randy was smart. He earned straight As, was admired by the teacher, and was never wrong. I was convinced. I would go home and announce to my dad that I was "on strike" until treated fairly.

I decided to wait for the right moment to make my announcement. Perhaps the following Saturday when he reminded me to mow the grass would be the right time. Sure enough, just as he always did, Dad stepped into my room with the usual reminder, "Don't forget to mow the lawn today, son."

"No," I said haughtily. Then, pausing for effect, I stared at him insolently and added, "I'm on strike. Also, I want an allowance starting now."

That was the first time I had ever told my dad no . . . and the last. Like Pearl Harbor, it was a day that would live in infamy.

After making sure he had heard me clearly, Dad gave me my next lesson in economics. "There are two things you need to know, boy," he said through fiery eyes and a menacing stare. "One is that you will do your chores as long as you live in this house. And two is that you never, ever tell me no."

> That was the first time I had ever told my dad no . . . and the last.

Then he took off his belt and the lesson went to a new level. I could have killed Randy. In fact, if I could find him today I would hurt him. Needless to say, the strike ended and my motivation to work around the house received a real boost. For some strange reason, to this day I get a nervous twitch when I put on my belt.

We began discussing Proverbs 29:18 in the last chapter. The verse tells us that where there is no vision or dream, we will perish. The word from which perish comes, *para*, is rich with meaning. We saw the following three definitions in the previous chapter: *unbridled, unprotected,* and *unready* for opportunity. Let's look now at a few more results of being dreamless.

The fourth meaning of *para* is "to withdraw." In Exodus 5:4, *para* is used in the context of withdrawing from or being *unwilling* to work. When I was a kid, Dad motivated me to work with the threat of pain. Now that I'm an adult, my heavenly Dad wants to motivate me with a dream. He knows that lacking a dream will cause me to be *unmotivated*.

It may come as a surprise to you that the greatest motivator in life is not need. If that were the case, the most motivated people would always be those on welfare. Sadly, this sometimes isn't the case. Without a dream to work toward, and with someone else to provide for them, welfare recipients are often unmotivated and unwilling to work.

Typically, the hardest worker in a company, at least in the start-up days, is the owner of the dream, not his employees. There is no greater motivator to hard work than a dream.

> **There is no greater motivator to hard work than a dream.**

Wilma Rudolph was the twentieth of twenty-two children. She was born prematurely and her survival was doubtful. When she was four, she contracted double pneumonia, scarlet fever, and polio, which left her with a paralyzed left leg. But Wilma had a dream. At age nine she removed the metal brace she had been dependent on and began to walk without it. By thirteen she had developed a rhythmic walk, which doctors said was a miracle.

It wasn't. Miracles are sudden, supernatural events accomplished by God and by Him alone. That wasn't His plan for Wilma. He wanted her to dream of walking without a brace and, through courage, tenacity, and hard work, to chase her dream. How else could she model greatness for the rest of us?

But walking wasn't enough for Wilma. That same year she decided to become a runner. I suppose if you're going to dream, you may as well go for the gold! She entered a race and came in last. For the next few years every race she entered, she came in last. Would the dream survive? Everyone told her to quit, but Wilma kept on running.

One day she broke her "sound barrier"—she actually won a race. And then another. From then on she won every race she entered. Eventually this little girl, who had been told she would never walk again, went on to win three Olympic gold medals. "My mother taught me very early to believe I could achieve any accomplishment I wanted to," Wilma explained. "The first was to walk without braces."[1]

Thank you, Wilma, and thank you, Mom, for demonstrating the power of a dream. Wilma took off a brace and strapped on a dream. Dreams heal. Or maybe they just motivate the Healer.

The fifth thing that can occur when we're without a dream came as somewhat of a surprise when I discovered it. *Para* is used elsewhere in Scripture to describe rejecting counsel (see Proverbs 1:25; 8:33; 13:18; 15:32). Interesting. Where there is no vision people are *unteachable*.

Perhaps the opposite is easier to see. One who is pursuing a dream is constantly looking for new and fresh ideas to help them on their journey. They realize that "without consultation, plans are frustrated, but with many counselors, they succeed" (Proverbs 15:22). Proverbs 20:18 tells us to "prepare plans by consultation." The wise dreamer knows the importance of this and pursues wisdom, counsel, and creative new ideas.

A stubborn, arrogant, and very obstinate man I met years ago embodied the concept of being unteachable. He made lots of money and had a beautiful wife and three wonderful children, but he was one of the most selfish individuals I had ever known. Over the years, people had tried to address his attitudes and issues, only to be rejected and insulted.

Then one day things began to unravel. His business was suffering, his kids were rebellious, and his wife had had enough of his cruel, selfish ways. She told him she was leaving.

This individual did something few men in his condition are willing to do: He took a long and honest look into his own heart. The only truthful conclusion was that his problems were self-inflicted. In a move that surprised everyone, he sought help. Over the next weeks and months he ruthlessly dealt with his issues. Allowing the Lord—with the help of a wise, discerning counselor—to break his hard, prideful heart, he was able to truly change and eventually win back his wife and kids. Ultimately, his business also recovered and once again he became very prosperous. When asked what it was that finally opened his heart to receive instruction and produce a willingness to change, his response was profoundly simple: "That's easy. It was the dream of having my family back."

Dreams soften the heart and open the mind.

The sixth and final definition of *para* relates especially to two or more people sharing a dream. Though corporate dreams are not our primary subject in this book, they are certainly worth mentioning. Leaders, especially, will find it interesting and helpful. *Para* means to let down or *unbraid* hair. To unbraid is to separate or *unravel*. Where there is no common vision, people disconnect. Commonality of cause and vision, however, brings people and their labors together. Whether the context is world evangelization, civil rights, saving babies, or saving whales, shared dreams motivate people to forget their differences and work for the cause.

I remember the first few days after 9/11. For a short and wonderful respite, there were no Republicans or Democrats, rich or poor, Protestants or Catholics. We were all simply Americans, united by the vision of caring for the hurting, protecting our nation, and administering justice to the perpetrators of the attack against us. Predictably, when the pain wore off, our differing agendas and "vision" caused us to unravel once more.

When God created us with our dreaming nature, He knew how powerful a force it would be. He was also very aware of the crippling results of losing this precious gift. He stands ready to lead each of us into the purposes He created us for and to birth in us the vision sufficient to accomplish them. And as we shall see, He has already placed within us the gifts and abilities we will need to succeed.

Take Gracie Mae, for example. . . .

For Review

1. What is the greatest motivation toward hard work? Explain.

2. Think about Wilma Rudolph's story. Try to imagine the challenges she had to overcome to walk and, eventually, run. Where can you apply similar perseverance in your life?

3. Explain how a lack of vision can cause us to be unteachable.

4. Think of a time when a dream caused you to be more hungry for, or open to, instruction.

5. How are the braiding of hair and dreams related?

8

Hounds and Roosters

Ceci and I have a Treeing Walker Coonhound. Not in a pen or running around the farm we don't have—in our house, in a quiet neighborhood. She was found in a cage at the local PetSmart, needing a home. My sweet wife, who it seems has the God-given destiny of seeing how many dogs one couple can own in a lifetime, swears she was providentially led to Gracie Mae. (All of Ceci's dogs have middle names.)

In fairness to Ceci, she texted me and asked if I was okay with her bringing home a puppy to join our other two spoiled dogs—on her way home with Gracie! I was beginning my texting dialogue with her as they walked in. Ceci was grinning; Gracie Mae, of course, was peeing. And so, another canine entered the Sheets "kennel." I've nicknamed our house The Ark.

We didn't know Gracie was a coon dog at first, just that she was a hound ("with a cute heart-shaped freckle on her nose"—Ceci). About two weeks into her adoption she found her bark. Correction: She doesn't bark—our other two dogs bark. Gracie howls or bays.

(Not being a coonhound expert, I looked up the word *bay* to make certain it was accurate: "a deep prolonged howl, as of a hound on a scent." Perfect.) When she made her first attempt at it, I said to Ceci, "That sounded like a coon dog." A couple weeks later the vet confirmed it—a Treeing Walker Coonhound.

Now that Gracie is fully grown, so is her howl. I've tried to come up with a spelling for how it sounds but can't. Just try to imagine Scooby Doo with a bullhorn. And when she talks—yes, she talks— it's simply a howl at a conversational volume. Sometimes she tries it with a bone in her mouth. She knows if she drops it one of the other two dogs might snatch it up, so she simply greets me with it in her mouth. Sounds like Scooby Doo with the croup.

We love Gracie Mae. We even like her howls and love language. She was born and bred to do it. It doesn't matter to Gracie that she's not in the woods treeing a coon; she was born to howl so she does it anyway.

When God wove us in our mothers' wombs He gave us our "howl." He placed certain bents, motivations, gifts, and abilities in us. Ephesians 2:10 tells us: "We are His workmanship, created in Christ Jesus for good works, which God prepared beforehand so that we would walk in them." Because we don't often use the term *workmanship* in our culture, this translation doesn't adequately communicate to us the strength of what God is saying. It doesn't simply mean that He created us. *Poiema,* the Greek word used here, means "a product," often referring to fabric or an outfit of clothing. This verse is using the same symbolism as Psalm 139:19, which says God "wove" us in our mother's womb. We are pieces of clothing, designed by God, that He intends to wear!

Consistent with this symbolism, the phrase "prepared beforehand" in this verse comes from a sewing term meaning "to measure or fit in advance." Like any good tailor, before God "wove" us in our mother's womb, He "measured" us. As our Creator and Destiny-giver, He made sure our gifts, abilities, personality, and motivations would fit our purpose. With these things in mind, qualities matching calling, He tailored us as the garment He would need to wear—He does live inside of us—in order to accomplish His purposes in and through us.

Poiema doesn't only refer to producing clothing, however. The words *poet*, *poem*, and *performer* also spring from the same root word. Using those analogies, the verse would say God is the performer and we're the song. He's the poet and we're the poem. If we don't allow the One who made us to influence our hopes and plans, life won't rhyme; we'll be out of rhythm. Dare I say, we'll be out of sync. We may even allow outside forces, adverse circumstances, or other people to write our story.

God warns us in Romans 12:2 not to allow outside agents to shape or design us. In this passage He does something very interesting, using the term *metamorphosis*, the transition of a caterpillar to a butterfly, to describe our transformation. In this analogy, the worm isn't being changed from the outside in but is "morphing" into what is *already programmed into its DNA*. The point couldn't be clearer: Make sure your dreams match your design—become who you are, not who you aren't!

> **Our Creator and Destiny-giver made sure our gifts, abilities, personality, and motivations would fit our purpose.**

No one who knew him well thought David, one of Israel's kings and ancient ancestor of Christ, was fit to be a king. I'm certain they didn't think he was a giant-slayer, either. When the prophet Samuel was sent to David's father, Jesse, to anoint one of his sons as the next king of Israel, David wasn't even invited to the choosing ceremony.

Had it not been for a "tuned in" prophet who realized the real king hadn't arrived yet, history might be very different. What might we call "the tabernacle of David"? Would Christ still be called "the

Son of David"? And who would have shown us what a "man after God's heart" looks like?

David's father thought he was only cut out to be a shepherd and errand boy. His brothers thought he was an arrogant runt hungry for attention. God's thesis on David said he was a history maker, a warrior, a worshiper. He "wove" him accordingly, writing in his heart dreams of nobility, strength, psalm writing, and radical worship.

Look deep inside and ask yourself what dreams God hid in you.

Aren't you glad David dreamed the right dreams? Most likely, more people have found comfort and solace from his words than any other. What would we have done without the Twenty-third Psalm? The Lord Himself quoted some of David's words while on the cross.

History is filled with similar what-ifs. What if Winston Churchill had believed his critics and chosen a different path? Would England have survived the onslaught of the Nazis without him? More than a century earlier, would the United States have survived and defeated the British if George Washington hadn't answered the call? Would there have been revivalists like John and Charles Wesley if Susanna, their mother, had adopted a different view of motherhood?

Look deep inside and ask yourself what dreams God hid in you. What makes you come alive? What strengths have lain dormant while you've pursued goals that could never fulfill you? Make a determination now to pursue the dreams God has for you.

In the *Pentecostal Evangel*, J. K. Gressett writes about a man named Samuel S. Scull, who settled on a farm in the Arizona desert with his wife and children:

One night, a fierce desert storm struck with rain, hail, and high wind. At daybreak, feeling sick and fearing what he might find, Samuel went to survey their loss. The hail had beaten the garden and truck patch into the ground; the house was partially unroofed; the hen house had blown away and dead chickens were scattered about. Destruction and devastation were everywhere.

While standing dazed, evaluating the mess and wondering about the future, he heard a stirring in the lumber pile that was the remains of the hen house. A rooster was climbing up through the debris and he didn't stop climbing until he had mounted the highest board in the pile. That old rooster was dripping wet, and most of his feathers were blown away. But as the sun came over the eastern horizon, he flapped his bony wings and proudly crowed.[1]

What a great example for us! The rooster knew his role. He wasn't trying to make a statement; nor was he checking to see if he could still do it. He was crowing simply because God put into his DNA the desire to announce the beginning of each new day. And nothing was going to change that. Sometimes animals seem to "get it" better than we humans.

Like our once fine-feathered friend, God made you with a purpose and inscribed it into your DNA. If you don't know what that purpose is, you could end up teaching school when your Designer needed and wove you to be an accountant. You might end up trapped in an office when the Writer needed and wanted a stay-at-home mom to help Him shape a child into a world-changer! Or perhaps you would pastor a congregation instead of being the CEO He created you to be. Many ill-fitted individuals have climbed to the top of debris piles and are trying to crow. They don't do it well and no one awakens to their sound.

What were you born to do? What did your Tailor measure you for? Are your dreams consistent with this? Is someone trying to make you act like a Yorkie when you're a bona fide Treeing Walker Coonhound? You will never be truly fulfilled until your dreams, goals, pursuits, and activities match what your Creator dreamed for you.

Like our canine friend, find your howl and be who you are meant to be. The first step is to believe God has a destiny for you. The second is to let Him into your dream mix. . . .

For Review

1. How might a baying coonhound be connected to destiny?

2. Explain the word *poiema* as it relates to our gifting.

3. Ephesians 2:10 tells us God "prepared beforehand" good works for us to accomplish. Expand the meaning of these words.

4. Write your own paraphrase of Ephesians 2:10 using the concepts we discussed in this chapter.

5. Describe traits you recognize in yourself that make you unique.

6. What gifts do you have that you aren't currently maximizing? What are you waiting for?

7. Are you wasting time and energy doing things that are not suited to your gifts? Think about how to change this.

9

The Dream Mix

During one of his lectures, Dr. George Washington Carver described the conversation with God that got him started studying the peanut. Most of us wouldn't have finished the conversation.

"Dear Creator, please tell me what the universe was made for?" he asked the Lord.

The Creator answered, "You want to know too much for that little mind of yours. Ask something more your size."

Many of us would have been offended and ended the dialogue there. But sometimes God uses extreme language simply to elicit the response He needs, not to offend.

Carver wasn't put off. Accepting the challenge, he replied, "Dear Creator, tell me what a man was made for."

Again the Lord replied, "Little man, you still ask too much. Cut down the extent of your request and improve your intent."

So then he asked, "Please, Mr. Creator, will you tell me why the peanut was made?"

"That's better," answered the Lord.

"And then the great Creator taught me how to take the peanut apart and put it back together again," stated the great Carver.

Kevin Shorter, in his book *Faith the Size of a Peanut*, says,

Dr. Carver revolutionized the southern agricultural economy by showing that 300 products could be derived from the peanut. The National Peanut Board reports Dr. Carver's works to include food products that ranged from chili sauce, caramel, mayonnaise and coffee. Cosmetics included face powder, shaving cream and hand lotion. Insecticides, glue, charcoal, rubber, and plastics are just a few of the many valuable peanut products discovered by Dr. Carver. By 1938 peanuts had become a $200 million industry and chief product of Alabama.[1]

I'm not sure what that figure would be today, almost seventy-five years later. A lot more, I know. Heck, my wife has spent that much alone on crunchy peanut butter, let alone all the cosmetics!

Since God gave us our dreaming nature, and since He has a purpose and destiny for each of us, it seems obvious He would want a voice in our choice of dreams. When this brilliant man, G. W. Carver, allowed God to choose his dream by humbling himself to ask for insight into the peanut, little did he know the impact it would have on the world.

There is a verse of Scripture that addresses this and has meant a great deal to Ceci and me over the years: "Roll your works on the Lord. Commit and trust them wholly to Him. *He will cause your thoughts to become agreeable to His will*, and so shall your plans be established and succeed" (Proverbs 16:3 AMP).

This wonderful verse seems almost too good to be true. God declares that He will supernaturally shape our thinking and plans, aligning them with His, which will then ensure success. *Plans* in this verse comes from a word meaning "to weave, plait, or mix." It can even refer to craftsmen inventing musical instruments, artistic objects, weapons, and other objects. The concept is simple: combining two or more substances to create something new. When used in reference to the mind, it refers to your thoughts mixing together to form plans. This obviously would include dreams.

Placing this definition back into the verse, God is saying to us: *When you dream, I want to be in the mix. If you will allow Me, I will infuse my thoughts into the process and shape your plans according to the purpose and destiny I have created for you. This will guarantee success.*

What a great promise!

I recall when Ceci and I were searching for the next phase of God's calling on our lives. We were recently married and I was about to graduate from Christ for the Nations Institute in Dallas. We had four opportunities with which to begin our world-changing ministry, the leading possibilities in our minds being overseas. We were standing on this verse, Proverbs 16:3 from the Amplified Bible.

We quoted the verse daily, usually picturing ourselves somewhere in Guatemala or Zimbabwe, preaching to thousands. Our bags were practically packed. Then something strange occurred. While praying one day I had the thought, *CFNI is going to offer you a position and you're to accept it.* This was nowhere on our radar!

Sure enough, within days the offer came and we said yes. It probably wouldn't surprise you to know that those next two years working at CFNI became invaluable preparation for what God has done through us the last thirty years. Proverbs 16:3 had worked: He infused His thoughts into ours and we listened, allowing Him "into the mix." Dreaming works out so much better when we bring the Author of dreams into the plans.

Proverbs 19:21 uses this same word: "Many *plans* are in a man's heart, but the counsel of the Lord will stand." Most of the time we humans make our plans and formulate our dreams without bringing God into the process. This began with Adam and Eve's original sin in Eden. Satan, the tempter, knew he could throw a wrench into God's dream by causing humans to dream without divine influence.

God didn't want a family of independent dreamers; He desired co-dreamers. It was never His plan that we dream apart from Him and His influence—not because He's a control freak, but because He wanted partners and associates. God wanted someone to dream *with* and someone to dream *through. He needed outlets for His dreams.*

In the first half of the twentieth century, God was dreaming some things about women and orphans in China. He was using Gladys Aylward.

In London in 1902, Gladys Aylward was born into a working-class family. After receiving salvation, she began reading books about the faraway land called China. At age twenty-eight, after being turned down by a missionary organization and feeling compelled to visit this land, she bought a one-way train ticket crossing Russia on her way to China.

God wanted someone to dream with and someone to dream through.

Gladys began her missionary career in Yangcheng. The local officials who asked if she would also become a "foot inspector" had huge respect for her. The tradition of binding Chinese women's feet had recently been outlawed but was still being practiced in many places. As she traveled and visited with the ladies, she would tell stories from the Bible, and many looked forward to the days they could hear these strange new stories. Gladys is credited with helping to change the foot-binding culture in China.

"The people's esteem and respect for Gladys continued to grow throughout the region," writes Ruth Tucker. Her ability to learn the Chinese culture and language was remarkable. By 1937, when the Japanese commenced bombing nearby mountain villages, she refused to leave when shells began to fall. "She even became a spy for the Chinese army using her foreign appearance to travel across battle lines and also bring food to trapped villagers. She was so effective that the Japanese put a price on her head.

"During this time Gladys also adopted war orphans and eventually had over 100 children in her care. In 1940, the war had escalated and she was forced to leave Northern China and head south to Sian through the thickening battle, over mountains and across the Yellow River. When Gladys climbed over the mountains to Sian, she had 100 children with her that she was taking to a refugee area. The journey took 12 days and they left with inadequate clothing or food, but God looked after Gladys and the children throughout the entire journey. . . .

"After 20 years in China," Tucker writes, "Gladys returned to England in 1940. She was embarrassed to find that she became a celebrity with a book, movie, and TV documentary being made about her life. To many, Gladys became known as 'The Small Woman,' the title of her biography."[2]

Gladys Aylward became an outlet for one of God's dreams. She was just an ordinary person with an extraordinary God who lifted her up to His level of dreaming, then empowered her to accomplish the dream. I wonder if she ever consciously thought that God was dreaming through her. He obviously was.

When we allow God to dream through us, we become His dream agents, representing Him and His plans on earth. This means that *hidden somewhere in one of God's dreams you'll discover those He has for you*—yours will be contained in His. The opposite is also true. *Hidden in your dreams, if they were given by Him, you'll find a piece of His.* This was and is His plan for all of us. Most people, however, go through life pursuing personal careers and goals without ever considering that God wants to dream through them. Too often, He's a lonely dreamer. There must be millions of written but unfulfilled destinies in God's dream book in heaven. The plans, accomplishments, and dreams He wrote about for so many are tragically undiscovered and unrealized. He and His plans never make it into their dream mix. Thankfully, this isn't always the case.

James Taylor, a chemist, was intrigued by all things Chinese, according to biographer Roger Steer. In the early months of 1832 Taylor knelt beside his wife, Amelia, in the parlor at the back of his busy chemist shop in Barnsley, Yorkshire, England. "Dear God," he prayed, "if you should give us a son, grant that he may work for you in China." When their child was born on May 21, 1832, James and Amelia called him James Hudson Taylor.

Immersed in a Methodist family fascinated with China, the young Hudson sometimes blurted out, "When I am a man, I mean to go to China," though his parents were not to tell him of their prayer for some years. He prepared himself by reading books on China, analyzing the Chinese gospel of Luke, and studying medicine. Finally, on September 19, 1853, Hudson left Liverpool harbor heading for China.

Taylor was concerned for the millions of Chinese living in provinces where no missionary had ever gone. In 1865, with great faith but limited financial resources, he founded the China Inland Mission with its goal being to present the gospel to all the provinces of China. By the time of Taylor's death in 1905, the CIM was an international body with 825 missionaries living in all eighteen provinces of China and twenty-five thousand Christian converts.

"Taylor stamped his own philosophy of life and work on the CIM. He required sole dependence on God financially with no guaranteed salary," writes another biographer, Ralph Covell, and Taylor insisted on close identification with the Chinese in their way of life.[3]

J. Hudson Taylor's parents put God into the mix of their dreams. Just as He promised in His Word, He infused His heart into theirs, and when they conceived a son, He stamped into his DNA the divine-human dream. Amazing. Only heaven knows the full extent of the fruit. Whether you become a missionary, an attorney, or a school-teacher, let God into your dreaming mix. Become the outlet for one of His dreams.

For Review

1. Explain Proverbs 16:3, especially the word *plans.*

2. How did George Washington Carver model this?

3. Give some thought to an area of your life in which you also could model this verse, allowing God "into the mix."

4. When did independent dreaming begin? How did this impart God's plans and desires?

5. Explain the phrase "we become His dream agents."

6. Have you determined that you will endeavor to bring God into your dreams? Are there selfish dreams in your heart you need to let go of?

7. Go back to your dreamorama. Do you see evidence that your dream contained part of His dream when you let Him influence it? As time progressed, did you see evidence of your dream in His? Give examples.

10

The Senior Partner

God is brilliant when it comes to hiding His dreams in the dreams of others. S. Truett Cathy, founder and chairman of Chick-fil-A, probably didn't know, initially, that this had happened to him. I, along with millions of cows (as we know from his advertising campaign), am glad for his dreams.

The restaurant's website says it all: "Armed with a keen business sense, a work ethic forged during the Depression and a personal and business philosophy based on biblical principles, Cathy took a tiny Atlanta diner, originally called the Dwarf Grill, and transformed it into Chick-fil-A, the nation's second largest quick-service chicken restaurant chain. His tremendous business success allowed Truett to pursue other passions—mostly notably his interest in the development of young people."

Cathy's WinShape Foundation, founded in 1984, grew from his desire to "shape winners" by helping young people succeed in life through scholarships and other youth-support programs. Each year the foundation awards scholarships to twenty to thirty students wishing to attend Berry College in Georgia. The foundation operates foster care homes in a number of states in the Southeast and in Brazil and also hosts almost two thousand campers each year through its WinShape Camps. These residential, two-week summer camps offer experiences to young people and families to enhance their Christian faith, character, and relationships.[1]

Would God really inspire an individual with a dream for a business such as this, then gift him with the ability to make it happen in order to satisfy His dreams for some orphans and students? Duh!—as we often say in response to the obvious. God loves slipping His dreams into ordinary people and then using them to bless others.

This is what happened to Abraham. He is one of my favorite Bible characters. I want to be like him—well, maybe not completely. I don't want to live in a tent, wouldn't have wanted to wait until I was one hundred to start my family, and hope I never offer Ceci to another man as his wife, telling him she is only my sister! But there are aspects of Abraham's life that inspire me, especially the fact that God ultimately called him His friend. I've thought about this often and simply can't imagine anything more fulfilling.

Abraham was also a dreamer, maybe one of the greatest ever. I think God liked that about him—at that time in history He needed a dreaming friend. The Lord had been waiting for just the right dreamer to come along, one He could partner with to recapture His dream. These two friends walked together for many years, enjoyed a special covenant with one another, and modeled for all of us the power and beauty of divine-human partnership. We will learn much about dreaming from this man and his journey with God. Their story begins in Genesis 12, where God initiates His plan by instilling a dream in Abraham.

Now the Lord said to Abram, "Go forth from your country, and from your relatives and from your father's house, to the land which I will show you; and I will make you a great nation, and I will bless you, and make your name great; and so you shall be a blessing; and I will bless those who bless you, and the one who curses you I will curse. And in you all the families of the earth will be blessed."

Genesis 12:1–3

It is fascinating that God began His journey with Abraham by appealing to his dreaming nature. The Lord's humility amazes me. Why, when looking for someone to help Him recapture His dream, would God need to offer anything? He is God, after all. Couldn't He have just forced Abraham do what He wanted? Possibly, but the Lord was well aware of the strength of the dreaming nature He placed within us. With this in mind, He knew that for the partnership to be fruitful and lasting, Abraham would have to be allowed to dream.

God doesn't expect us to ignore our strong desire to dream and, in fact, loves it when we do. His plan, therefore, is usually to inspire us with a personal dream, then infuse His into ours. With this in mind, God began placing a dream in Abraham's heart involving lands, material blessings, and ultimately the birthing of a great nation.

The problem is not (and never was) that God doesn't want us in His world of dreaming. His challenge is that we won't allow Him into ours. Trust isn't God's problem—it's ours. Since the Fall, we humans have had difficulty trusting God with our dreams. The irony of ironies is that we no longer allow the God who gave us our dreaming nature into the mix. We gladly ask Him to bless our personal dreams, but few of us will allow Him to influence the actual dreaming process. The twofold result of this is we often don't experience our destiny and God doesn't have outlets for His dreams.

Trust Him and He will dream wonderful and exciting dreams through you. And as this story illustrates, those who taste the awesomeness of this never go back to dreaming without him.

The Standard Oil Company was making preparations to establish itself in Indonesia. Company executives were seeking a manager for their operations. They were told that the best man for the job was a certain missionary. The company approached the missionary in reference to his availability for the position. They offered a large salary. The missionary declined. The company raised the offer. Still he declined. Finally they said, "Just name your salary." "Oh," replied the missionary, "the salary is big enough, but the job isn't."[2]

Once you start dreaming with God, you'll never want to stop. This addiction occurred with Abraham. His encounter with the Lord began a co-dreaming venture that lasted the rest of his life, the fruit of which remains today.

Having established the all-important fact that God was including Abraham in the dreaming process, two more very important principles concerning dreaming are revealed in their inaugural meeting. The first of them is that when we become dreaming partners with God, *He must always be the Senior Partner.*

Jehovah was inviting Abram into His world, not vice versa. He is the Lord and Creator; we are the created. He's the leader—we follow His leading. Though doing so with great promise of blessing to Abraham, God is obviously the one seen offering the terms and conditions: "Go to the land I will show you . . . I will make you . . . I will bless you . . . I will bless those who bless you, and the one who curses you I will curse" (Genesis 12:1–3). Twice in the passage Abraham is seen building altars and worshiping the Lord. This demonstrates clearly his devotion and submission to Jehovah. The arrangement is clear: God, the Senior Partner, is offering a conditional partnership to Abraham, not the other way around. The rewards for Abraham were great, but only if he chose God's terms and conditions.

So often we try to reverse this, acting as though we're doing God a favor by allowing Him into our dreaming world, even going so far as to approach Him in a deal-making manner: "If you do this for me, God, I will . . ." We sometimes even use phrases that suggest we're giving God a try, or that we're inviting *Him* into *our* world.

We offer Him token pieces of our dreams, time, money, and desires, all the while acting as though we're doing Him a favor.

This unbiblical mindset sets the course for a relationship with God that relegates Him to a Junior Partner position. We must remember that it is His grace that causes Him to accept and invite us into His world. Though He is not condescending toward us—as a loving Father He treats us with amazing love and grace—nonetheless, He is God, not a peer.

> **Our loving Father treats us with amazing love and grace— nonetheless, He is God, not a peer.**

The other important principle shown to us in Genesis 12 is that *dreaming requires risk-taking.* It took a huge risk and great faith on Abraham's part to pursue the dream God was offering. Yahweh refused to give him many details up front, even refusing to tell him where He was leading him. "You just go, Abraham, and I'll lead you along the way. Pack everything and follow me."

What a challenge! The faith this required was incredible and for Abraham the risks were monumental: *What if I'm not hearing God correctly,* or, *What if this isn't Him talking to me at all?* To Abraham, however, the dream was worth the risk! He took the chance, and God never forgot the trust he demonstrated. The Holy Spirit was still thinking about it hundreds of years later when He inspired the book of Hebrews.

> By faith Abraham, when he was called, obeyed by going out to a place which he was to receive for an inheritance; and he went out, not knowing where he was going.
>
> Hebrews 11:8

Those who need the comfort of the familiar or the security of the known can forget dreaming. The leap of faith will always be a bit too unsettling. They're like the African gazelle, which can jump fairly high and up to thirty feet in distance. In spite of this, they can be confined in zoos with only a three-foot wall. The reason: Gazelles won't jump if they can't see where they will land. We are often like the gazelle, blessed with great ability and potential, yet imprisoned by the fear of the unknown.

Predictability and mapped-out routes are for nondreamers and Google Maps. Dreamers, on the other hand, will be found heading into the unknown, going out on a limb, and at times hanging by a thread. Pick your own risk cliché, just know you'll have to do it. But when God is the source of the dream, that makes Him the limb, the thread, and the guide into the unknown. True faith is not reckless-ness. It does, however, require a willingness to risk, as the late Steve Jobs demonstrated.

> When Apple Computer fell on difficult days a while back, Apple's young chairman, Steven Jobs, traveled from the Silicon Valley to New York City. His purpose was to convince Pepsico's John Sculley to move west and run his struggling company.
>
> As the two men overlooked the Manhattan skyline from Sculley's penthouse office, the Pepsi executive started to decline Jobs's offer.
>
> "Financially," Sculley said, "you'd have to give me a million-dollar salary, a million-dollar bonus, and a million-dollar severance."
>
> Flabbergasted, Jobs gulped and agreed—if Sculley would move to California. But Sculley would commit only to being a consultant from New York. At that, Jobs issued a challenge to Sculley: "Do you want to spend the rest of your life selling sugared water, or do you want to change the world?"
>
> In his autobiography *Odyssey*, Sculley admits Jobs's challenge "knocked the wind out of me." He said he'd become so caught up with his future at Pepsi, his pension, and whether his family could adapt to life in California that an opportunity to "change the world" nearly passed him by. Instead, he put his life in perspective and went to Apple.[3]

Changing the world always requires the inconvenience of change and the unsettledness of risk. Abraham took this risk and, though he didn't know it at the time, stepped into the greatest partnership imaginable: working with God to save the world. "In you," the Lord told Abraham, "all the families of the earth will be blessed" (Genesis 12:3). Though I'm certain he didn't fully understand the phrase, in hindsight it is clear. *If you'll trust Me with your future, Abraham, I'll let you in on Mine. You can be My partner in redeeming the world—the Messiah will come through you!*

Incredible! Dreaming with God to save the world!

In His quest to redeem the world back to Himself, God is still looking for partners. He places dreams in human hearts, then discreetly hides one of His next to it. He *always* has a dream hidden in the dreams He gives to us. If being a stay-at-home mom is a dream of yours, rest assured God has great plans for those kids. Why not elevate your dream of raising children to that of producing God-partners?

If your dream is to make great sums of money, why would you want to do so only to enjoy it for a few short years? Why not partner with God through your money, and by doing so lay up treasure in heaven where you can enjoy it forever? And why settle only for human gifts and abilities with which to make money, when you could partner with the One who created everything and has unlimited resources?

Whatever your God-given dream, look for one of His hidden inside. It's there. Once this reality is discovered it changes our thinking. Our dreams are elevated to a heavenly perspective, and we now see them as having eternal significance. This allows God to become more involved in their fulfillment, bringing supernatural favor and blessing to our efforts. And with Him as our partner, anything is possible.

For Review

1. List the three principles concerning dreaming that were revealed in God and Abraham's co-dreaming venture.

2. Why did God appeal to Abraham's dreaming nature?

3. Explain the Senior Partner/Junior Partner concepts in this chapter. Describe your partnership with God. Has it grown to include the dreaming process? What position do you consistently give God in the partnership?

4. Are there dreams in your heart you have refused to allow God control of?

5. How did Abraham model risk-taking? What is your capacity to take risks? Have you gone out on His limb while partnering in the dream? Name occasions when you have done this.

6. How can you make God's dream a more important part of yours?

11

Choices

"W hy have we stopped here, Uncle Caleb?" Othniel might have asked. "We were doing so well in our campaign to take the Promised Land. And why make everyone, including the women and kids, pull up camp and journey here to Shechem? It's an interesting place, nestled between Mount Ebal and Mount Gerizim, but it sure was a challenge getting here."

"I'm not sure, but it has something to do with our history concerning Abraham and Moses," answered Caleb. "This was the first place Yahweh brought Abraham after promising him the land. And before he died, Moses made Joshua promise to bring the entire nation here as soon as enough of the land had been taken to make it safely possible. Joshua has already sent six delegates from six of the tribes to Ebal; the other six delegates are headed to Gerizim. They're climbing the mountains now. I suppose we'll know what this is all about soon enough."

Without warning, the sound of a ram's horn pierced the silence in Shechem valley, calling Israel to attention. As they waited, one of

the six delegates on Ebal stepped onto an overhang facing Shechem
and with a loud voice began to declare,

> "Cursed is the man who makes an idol or a molten image, an abomi-
> nation to the Lord. . . . Cursed is he who dishonors his father or
> mother . . . he who moves his neighbor's boundary mark . . . he who
> misleads a blind person on the road . . . he who distorts the justice
> due an orphan, and widow . . . he who lies with his father's wife . . .
> he who strikes his neighbor in secret . . . he who accepts a bribe to
> strike down an innocent person. . . . Cursed is he who does not con-
> firm the words of this law by doing them."
>
> portions of Deuteronomy 27:15–26

These solemn and sobering announcements went on for several
minutes as the people listened intently.

"Whoa, that was intense," whispered Othniel when the warnings
stopped.

"You think that was intense?" answered Caleb. "You should've
been around when the earth opened and swallowed Korah and his
rebellious followers. That was intense. Or when the Red Sea swallowed
Pharaoh and his army. So far, this isn't too bad." Othniel loved hearing
Uncle Caleb tell stories of the exodus—the plagues, the pillar of fire,
Sinai rumbling, and many others. Caleb, it seemed, had seen it all.

Then, as the people were pondering at the curses shouted from
Ebal, someone began to shout from Mount Gerizim:

> "Now it shall be, if you will diligently obey the Lord your God, being
> careful to do all His commandments which I command you today, the
> Lord your God will set you high above all the nations of the earth.
>
> "And all these blessings shall come upon you and overtake you
> if you obey the Lord your God: Blessed shall you be in the city, and
> blessed shall you be in the county. Blessed shall be the offspring of
> your body and the produce of your ground . . . your beasts . . . your
> herd . . . your basket. . . .

"Blessed shall you be when you come in and blessed shall you be when you go out. The Lord shall cause your enemies who rise up against you to be defeated before you; they will come out against you one way and will flee before you seven ways. The Lord will command the blessing upon you in your barns and in all that you put your hand to, and He will bless you in the land which the Lord your God gives you."

portions of Deuteronomy 28:1–14

On and on the blessings resulting from obedience echoed across the valley. Though only a few minutes, it seemed like an hour. Then, just as the people began to relax, another volley rang out from Ebal:

"But it shall come about, if you will not obey the Lord your God . . . all these curses shall become upon you and overtake you. Cursed shall you be in the city, and cursed shall you be in the country. . . . Cursed shall be your basket . . . your offspring . . . your produce . . . your herd. . . . Cursed shall you be when you come in, and . . . when you go out.

"The Lord will send upon you curses, confusion . . . pestilence . . . consumption . . . fiery heat . . . the sword . . . plagues . . . sicknesses. . . . So all these curses shall come on you and pursue you and overtake you until you are destroyed because you would not obey the Lord your God by keeping His commandments and His statutes which He commanded you. They shall become a sign and a wonder on you and your descendants forever."

portions of Deuteronomy 28:15–68

It didn't seem like the list of curses would ever end. No one spoke for several minutes, until finally Caleb soberly addressed Othniel and the rest of his family gathered around him. "That did get a little intense, didn't it? Well, we can't say we weren't warned." Then, after thinking quietly for a moment, he added, "So that's why God brought Abraham to this place first."

"Why's that, Caleb?"

"To offer him a *choice*, just like He has with us here today. The promise of the land, and of being a holy nation through whom God would reveal Himself to the world—this came to Abraham with conditions, and it's being offered to us with conditions, as well. *Disobedience will curse the dream, obedience will bless it.*"

From that day forward, Gerizim became known as the "Mount of Blessings" and Ebal—with even its barren, lifeless terrain picturing what it symbolized—became the "Mount of Cursing." Shechem, the city in between, became the "Place of Choosing."

The Lord would end up leading Abraham to many places on his dream journey. Many of them would be significant, some more than others. Abraham would build an altar at only four of them, however—a practice which unmistakably marked those places as some of the most significant on his dream journey. Shechem was first (see Genesis 12:6). Sandwiched between the mountains of blessing and cursing, it would forever state the obvious: Obedience keeps the dream connected to God and His blessing; disobedience brings a disconnection from Him, which will always curse it.

When you think about it, that's what Adam did—he disconnected the dream from God through disobedience. How logical, then, that God would begin the dream journey with Abraham, and later all of Israel, here. He was showing them that *the first step to possessing their dream was staying connected to the Lord of the dream!*

The results of obeying versus disobeying can be huge:

A TV news camera crew was on assignment in southern Florida filming the widespread destruction of Hurricane Andrew.

In one scene, amid the devastation and debris stood one house on its foundation. The owner was cleaning up the yard when a reporter approached him.

"Sir, why is your house the only one still standing?" asked the reporter. "How did you manage to escape the severe damage of the hurricane?"

"I built this house myself," the man replied. "I also built it according to the Florida state building code. When the code called for 2x6 roof trusses, I used 2x6 roof trusses. I was told that a house built according to code could withstand a hurricane. I did, and it did. I suppose no one else around here followed the code."[1]

Like these building codes, obedience to God isn't meant to oppress us, but to protect us. He wants our dream protected and blessed as much as we do. Obedience keeps it tethered to Him and safe from the inevitable storms that will try to destroy it.

Years later, Joshua is again seen reminding Israel of this principle (see Joshua 24). After Israel had conquered their enemies and lived in the Promised Land for several years, compromise had begun to creep in. Bad choices were being made, other gods were being served and worshiped. Ebal, the mountain of cursing, was being chosen. Joshua, now an old man, felt the need to warn Israel one last time before his departure to paradise. *Where should I give my impassioned speech?* he probably wondered. As he considered the list of significant places—and there were many—one location just seemed to stand out.

Shechem.

> **Obedience to God isn't meant to oppress us, but to protect us.**

Once again Joshua gathered the nation to this historical and holy place between the emblematic mountains and gave his impassioned speech. He began by recounting their glorious history and the wonderful promises God had made to them. "We're living the dream others worked so hard for and waited so long to see," he reminded them. "Many never even made it this far—they saw it only by faith."

Perhaps he then reminded them of the awesome ceremony years ago, pointing first at Ebal, then Gerizim. He ended his eloquent speech by reminding them they must choose obedience in order to experience God's blessing. Then with fire in his eyes and determination in his voice, Joshua made his famous and often quoted declaration: "Choose for yourselves today whom you will serve. . . . As for me and my house, we will serve the Lord" (Joshua 24:15).

These immortalized words must forever be the dreamer's creed! We must not serve our flesh, other gods, or even the dream itself. We must serve Him! It is of little wonder that God took Abraham to Shechem at the beginning of their journey. All who wish to dream with Him must go there, where we are reminded once and for all that our choices bless or curse the dream.

Most of us have seen the movie *Annie*, the story of a spunky, red-haired girl who dreams of life outside her orphanage. Eleven-year-old Annie has been living in an orphanage her whole life. One day, she is chosen to stay for a week with a billionaire named Oliver "Daddy" Warbucks. Annie wins his heart and Warbucks decides to adopt her.

In Disney's 1999 remake of this heartwarming story, Annie's astonishment when first seeing Warbucks' palatial home is humorous. In her typical flare and dramatic style, Annie takes it all in and then exclaims, "Leapin' lizards, look at this joint!"

Sometimes I wonder what our response will be when we see "Dad's" house in heaven. Probably not "leapin' lizards," but I can't help but believe there will be some humorous exclamations.

Abraham's second stop on his dream journey was God's house. Well, maybe not the real one, but a town whose name, Bethel, meant "house of God." And like Annie's good fortune of being brought into Daddy Warbucks's house and family, this town was meant to symbolize for us the blessing of becoming members of God's household.

In order to properly paint the picture He wanted us to see, the Artist led Abraham to camp just east of town. This placed him between Bethel and the small town of Ai, which means "a heap of ruins." Leapin' lizards, what a horrible name! I'm not sure why anyone would give their town a depressing name like Ai, but it certainly works well for the symbolism God was about to use.

It doesn't require a lot of prophetic insight to see that by leading Abraham to camp with "God's house" on one side and "a heap of ruins" on the other, the Lord was once again offering Abraham a choice. There was a major difference, however, between this offer and the one pictured at Shechem. At Shechem he had to choose the Lord as his *God*; at Bethel, he chose Him as *Father*.

Being offered a membership in God's house meant that God was extending to Abraham the privilege and benefits of family. "Choose to live with Me and experience the blessings of My household, Abraham, or experience the ruin and destruction of life without Me." Talk about a no-brainer!

As wonderful as it is to become part of God's household, Bethel shows us something even more meaningful. God's ultimate plan was not only for us to *live in* His house but to *be* His house—after the cross, those who accept Christ become Bethel! In recapturing His dream, God wouldn't stop until He was once again able to breathe His Spirit into our spirits, making us His dwelling place.

When the apostle Paul said we are now the temple of the Holy Spirit (see 1 Corinthians 3:16; 6:19), the word he used for temple was a term reserved only for the Holy of Holies in Solomon's temple. This was the inner sanctuary where the presence and glory of God dwelled. Incredibly, he was saying we had become the Holy of Holies and the shekinah glory of God now dwelled in us—we had become Bethel.

This changes everything about our dreaming! God can now birth dreams *from within* us, not just influence them *from without*. And to accomplish our dreams we don't have to rely only on our own limited understanding, wisdom, and abilities. The Holy Spirit within us will act as our counselor and guide. The Dream-giver is now our Dream-coach. Shechem and Bethel revealed to Abraham that his God and Father was waiting to bless the dream. Our heavenly Father loves us, and He loves it when we dream. As long as we choose to walk with Him, He is ready to bless and guide us into successful dreaming.

But, as Abraham would discover, there is still another level to our relationship with our Creator.

For Review

1. Describe the location of Shechem and the significance of this.

2. What is the first step to possessing the dream?

3. Where did Joshua give his famous speech recorded in Joshua 24? Why?

4. Describe the location of Bethel and the significance of where it was located.

5. What is the meaning of "Bethel"? What does this mean to us?

6. Think about how the important truths from Shechem and Bethel could apply to your life and dreams. Be honest. Are all your dreams tethered to Him? Do you know Him as Father or do you live like an orphan?

12

Dreaming With Friends

I called myself a Christian for seventeen years before I discovered I could have a truly personal relationship with God. Prior to this, I certainly knew Him as God and I definitely knew Him as my Savior. I did not, however, know Him as my Father, and walking with Him as a friend wasn't even in the field of view. Satan and his team, with lots of help from religion, have painted God as a very distant, non-relational being. If thought of at all, our Creator is primarily considered the Judge or, in times of crisis, a possible but unlikely means of help. Our adversary is nothing if not a very skilled deceiver.

After Adam's fall, Abraham's journey with God was the first and probably the most in-depth revelation of the type of relationship He desired with us. Let's review. Their journey together began at Shechem, which illustrated God's dream of ending man's rebellion and demonstrated the blessing of choosing Him as our God.

Bethel took things to another level. Yahweh had much more in mind than simply being our God. His dream was to enjoy us as family and to make us His abode again. There we chose Him not just as our God but also as our Father. At Bethel, the Dream-giver became the Dream-guide.

By the time we get to the thirteenth chapter of Genesis, Abraham and God had walked together for quite some time. The Lord had upheld His end of the deal and prospered Abraham greatly; he was now rich in cattle, silver, and gold (see Genesis 13:2). Due to his nomadic lifestyle he had roamed to several different locations, then decided to make a return visit to Bethel. While there, he and the Lord reminisced concerning their beginning (see Genesis 13:4), and Abraham listened as God encouraged him to keep the dream alive:

> The Lord said to Abram, after Lot had separated from him, "Now lift up your eyes and look from the place where you are, northward and southward and eastward and westward; for all the land which you see, I will give it to you and to your descendants forever. I will make your descendants as the dust of the earth so that if anyone can number the dust of the earth, then your descendants can also be numbered. Arise, walk about the land through its length and breadth; for I will give it to you."
>
> Genesis 13:14–17

At this time, Abraham decided to move again and relocate to Hebron, the third place where he built an altar. "Then Abram moved his tent and came and dwelt by the oaks of Mamre, which are in Hebron, and there he built an altar to the Lord" (Genesis 13:18). The meaning of this city's name, Hebron, holds the concept of a close connection or relationship such as a league, federation, association, or *friendship*. This small town high upon a hill took Abraham's walk with God to an entirely new level.

We're not told the reasoning behind Abraham's choosing the time and place for this move. Was it his choice? Was it God's? Knowing the Lord as I do, and observing the way He so carefully directed Abraham on his journey, I believe He led Abraham to Hebron. The progression is too obvious. At Shechem Abraham chose the Lord as his *God*. At Bethel he chose Him as *Father* and they lived together as family. But what God had in mind all along was to mature the relationship into a friendship. *God wants to dream with friends.*

The thought of friendship with God is more than simply intriguing to me. It messes with me! It tugs at my heart and calls out to me. Like the natal homing of a sea turtle experiencing the invisible but irresistible pull to the place of its birth, it woos me. Somehow I know in the deepest part of my nature that it is my destination, my home. His desire for friendship was the place in His heart where we were conceived. Our quest and destiny is to find it again.

Friendship with Him *is* the dream.

A few years ago I was elk hunting in the mountains of Colorado when I saw a monument to friendship. High on a mountain, near the edge where one of the most majestic views imaginable could be seen, was a plaque encased in a rock. Tears came to my eyes as I read the words carved into the plaque:

> In memory of my friend and hunting partner,
> [name], with whom I roamed these mountains
> from 1963–2003. He loved these mountain, streams,
> snow packed peaks and beautiful valleys.
> I miss him.
>
> [Name]
> 1930–2003

It may sound overly dramatic, but I removed my hat and stood in silence, saluting the friendship enjoyed by these men. I tried to imagine the joys and memories created, as well as the pain of the loss he must have felt as an old warrior climbed this hill, memorial in hand, to honor the memory of a true friend. One can only imagine the hours they shared together. The only way to truly understand the camaraderie that develops when friends share the wonder and awe of creation together is to experience it. I thought of this as I stood looking over the vastness of the Rocky Mountains. Then I thought how much greater is the awesomeness of sharing moments such as these with the Creator Himself.

Abraham didn't begin his journey as the friend of God, nor do we. It is possible to find Bethel, to be in God's family, and not be His friend just as it is with our natural family. We can be in the same family with a person, even as their son or daughter, and not be friends. A friendship implies closeness and takes time to develop. It is comprised of trust, compatibility, affection, and, of course, a high level of interpersonal knowledge.

I have many acquaintances but very few people I call my friends. The few that I classify as such are those I enjoy spending quality time with, sharing life's experiences together. We're vulnerable with one another, freely communicating our hopes and dreams. I celebrate my victories with them and am comforted by them when I'm hurting. We keep it real. My walls are down when we're together; I'm unguarded and transparent, unafraid to let them see the real me—the unpolished version. I know they will always "be there" for me and I for them. Many more defining characteristics of friendship could be stated, but this much is clear: Friendship defines the highest level of relationship.

I'm sometimes amused when I hear the average Christian reference God as their "friend." There was a popular chorus a few years back about being God's friend. I liked the song, but as I listened to crowds of people singing it, I couldn't help but think how untrue it was for most of them. I suppose it's good to sing it as a reminder of God's offer to us, just as my parents used to sing "What a Friend We Have in Jesus." These songs may be reality for those who wrote them, but for the average person singing them, they simply aren't true. Most Christians have no true intimacy with God, spend very little time with Him, and have a very limited knowledge of His heart and ways. "A casual acquaintance" would best define their relationship with Him. We mustn't cheapen friendship by lowering the standard.

I want to quickly point out, however, that friendship with God is possible for every believer and is His desire for us. This is the whole point of Hebron. God eventually enjoyed this level of relationship with Abraham—three times in Scripture He called him His friend—and it's what He desires with each one of us. This is not only a part of our destiny, it's part of God's dream.

In exposing our shallow understanding of friendship with God and the fact that so few experience it, I don't mean to impugn our intentions and motives. The fact is, we're much like Abraham was at the beginning of his journey with the Lord. Most of us begin our walk with God just as he did—wanting the benefits He offers. We aren't terribly interested in His dreams; we probably aren't even consciously aware that He has any.

> **Friendship with God is possible for every believer and is His desire for us.**

But we are very aware that He can help us with our dreams, so we cut deals with Him, talk to Him primarily on the basis of our needs, and remind Him that He is our Father—our source.

In his sermon "The Disciple's Prayer," Haddon Robinson tells the following story which pictures this unenlightened and inappropriate beginning.

> When our children were small, we played a game. I'd take some coins in my fist. They'd sit on my lap and work to get my fingers open. According to the international rules of finger opening, once the finger was open, it couldn't be closed again. Then they would work at it, until they got the pennies in my hand. They would jump down and run away, filled with glee and delight. Just kids. Just a game.
>
> Sometimes when we come to God, we come for the pennies in His hand.
>
> "Lord, I need a passing grade. Help me to study."
>
> "Lord, I need a job."
>
> "Lord, I need a car."
>
> We reach for the pennies. Then we walk away.[1]

Do we initially see God as our Provider? Yes. Do we really know Him as a Friend? No, not at the beginning of our journey. God understands this, however, and in His love and humility is willing to meet us where we are. "He loves us first," the Scriptures tell us (1 John 4:19), not the other way around. His love embraces us and makes us His child. And just as a natural child doesn't begin its relationship on a friendship level with Mom and Dad, our heavenly Father knows we won't with Him either.

Most of us, when younger and in our parents' home, trusted them to provide for us. Appropriately so. But for most of us the day arrived when we wanted to be more than just a well-cared-for child. I know I did—I wanted to be my parents' friend. At that point I cared more about their happiness, well-being, and dreams than I did their money. I wanted to give to them more than I wanted to take from them. We no longer talked only about my happiness, we discussed things that interested them, as well. Over the years their faith had been transferred to me, and we dreamed together about making a difference for God. Our relationship had matured into a friendship.

The same was true of Abraham. He started his journey with God looking for lands, blessings, and greatness. He embraced the promise of a biological son through whom he would produce a great nation. But thankfully, the relationship grew. There were even some rough spots along the way. When God didn't provide the son He promised Abraham and Sarah in the way they expected, they demonstrated their lack of trust by choosing to have a son through Hagar, Sarah's maid.

But though Abraham demonstrated humanness, in the end he proved his trust in God had grown to a level few people ever attain. He was even willing to sacrifice Isaac, his long-awaited son, believing if he did so God would raise Isaac from the dead. What trust!

The Lord so cherished His friendship with Abraham that, when Abraham died, He saw to it Abraham was buried at Hebron. I can't help but believe that, like the hunting friend's mountaintop plaque, this was God's tribute to their friendship. Upon Abraham's arrival in heaven, I like to think perhaps Jehovah stood, got everyone's attention, and honored the old patriarch, "This is Abraham, my friend. We dreamed together."

When God is looking for someone in His family He can be vulnerable with, a friend with whom He can share His hopes, dreams, and, yes, even His disappointments, I hope He feels He can look to me. And when my life is over and my body laid to rest, if it can be said that He and I were friends, I will have been a success.

Let's go to Hebron.

For Review

1. God, Savior, Father, Friend—where do you fall on this list of knowing God?

2. Retrace Abraham's path of building altars from Shechem to Hebron. Compare your path with the markers on Abraham's.

3. Are you ready to go to Hebron? Set aside time with Him. Walk, pray, talk to Him. Commit and surrender to friendship—or deeper friendship—with Him. Journal this interaction with Him.

4. Think of someone you know who models friendship with God. What do you see in them that you can emulate?

5. What attitudes, weaknesses, or actions exist in your life that stand in the way of friendship with God? Repent of these and determine a path to overcome them.

13

Caleb

Hebron, with its rich history and prophetic symbolism, became such a significant city that it deserves another look. For generation after generation it remained one of the most important places in all of Israel.

Even though the Lord gave Abraham the family He had promised and blessed him materially until he was very wealthy, it took over four hundred years before full possession of all the lands actually happened. Obviously, this did not take place in Abraham's lifetime but ultimately occurred through his descendents and in-laws. One of them was a friend of God's named Caleb.

Caleb was a dreamer—and what a dreamer he was! This warrior was one of the twelve spies sent by Moses to spy out the Promised Land. He and his friend Joshua were the only two spies with enough faith and courage to believe Israel could defeat the giants and possess what God had promised. For the other ten, the risks outweighed the dream.

For every dreamer, there will always come a time when their dream is measured against the risks. There are giants standing in opposition to every worthwhile dream. Whether or not the risk is taken and the giant is faced will be determined by the value of the dream and the perceived odds of success.

In the movie *Braveheart*, William Wallace is challenging his brothers to not give up their dream of freedom. They are terrified of the powerful British army, badly outnumbered, and want to flee. Wallace, of course, is ready to "pick a fight." His question causes them to consider the value of the dream.

"I am William Wallace, and before me, I see a whole army of my countrymen here to battle the English. Ay, fight and you may die, run and you'll live. At least a while. And dying in your beds many years from now, would you be willing to trade all the days from this day to that for one chance, just one chance to come back here and tell our enemies that they may take our lives . . . but they'll never take our FREEDOM!!!"[1]

> **There are giants standing in opposition to every worthwhile dream.**

For Wallace, the decision was a no-brainer. The same was true of Caleb. The reward far outweighed the risks. The value of freedom from Egypt's slavery and the bounty of the Promised Land made the decision easy. His rock-solid faith in God made it even easier: "Let's go get the dream."

By the time Caleb and Israel went into the land promised to Abraham, the name of Hebron had changed. It was currently called Kiriath-Arba, which means "the city of Arba." Arba was the greatest of the giants inhabiting the land (see Joshua 14:15). This demonized giant had claimed the city for himself since it was the highest point in the land, and had established his rule there. Isn't it just like Satan to lay claim to and defile something that is special to God? He is always after God's dreams.

When spying out the land, Caleb had seen Kiriath-Arba, now occupied by this arrogant giant, and decided he wanted it for his hometown.

Perhaps he knew its history well enough to know that Abraham, the friend of God, was buried there. Or maybe the aspect of living in the place representing friendship with God was his attraction to it. Or then again, maybe he just didn't like mean giants! We don't know. What we do know is Caleb said, "I'm claiming that mountain. We're well able to defeat these giants and I'll take the biggest" (see Joshua 14:6–15).

Now there's a dreamer. A bold, risk-taking dreamer.

Of course, those of you who know the story realize that due to the fear and unbelief of the non-risk-takers, Caleb had to wait forty-five years to get his dream. The Lord made the unbelieving generation of Israelites wander in the desert forty years until they all died, then allowed the next generation to go in and possess the land. Though he had to wait a few decades, Caleb was given his dream. He conquered the descendants of Arba and took possession of this stronghold on the hill. And what did he rename "the city of the greatest giant"? Hebron, of course.

Caleb and his story have inspired millions of people over the last several centuries. Thousands of messages have been preached about this faith-filled dreamer, and rightfully so. What are some of the more important lessons we can draw from him that will help us on our dream journey? Here are a few obvious ones.

First, *never give up on dreaming*. As we grow older, dreams sometimes change but our dreaming nature shouldn't. Keep dreaming and, whenever possible, keep every dream alive. Caleb had to wait forty-plus years to receive his promise, but it was still worth it. And God supernaturally kept this warrior strong and in good health so he could possess it and enjoy living there. In Joshua 14:11, Caleb says, "I am still as strong today as I was in the day Moses sent me; as my strength was then, so my strength is now, for war and for going out and coming in." Caleb was eighty-five years old when he said this. God never forgets His promises to His friends.

Caleb also teaches us that *completely selling out to God and His cause results in dream fulfillment*. "Therefore, Hebron became the inheritance of Caleb the son of Jephunneh the Kenizzite until this day, because he followed the Lord God of Israel fully" (Joshua 14:14). God loves wholeheartedness. His testimony that Caleb followed Him fully is one of the greatest tributes that could ever be given to a person. Religion won't produce that type of devotion—only friendship. Or perhaps family.

> Alvin Straight, age seventy-three, lived in Laurens, Iowa. His brother, age eighty, lived several hundred miles away in Blue River, Wisconsin. According to the Associated Press, Alvin's brother had suffered a stroke and Alvin wanted to see him, but he had a transportation problem. He didn't have a driver's license because his eyesight was bad and he apparently had an aversion to taking a plane, train, or bus.
>
> But Alvin didn't let that stop him. In 1994 he climbed aboard his 1966 John Deere lawn mower and drove it all the way to Blue River, Wisconsin.
>
> Devotion finds a way.[2]

Alvin's wholehearted commitment and dream of seeing his brother overcame the obstacles. Likewise, Caleb's dream of seeing the Promised Land be fully possessed by Abraham's descendents, as well as his complete trust in and obedience to the One who first gave the dream, brought divine enablement. Caleb knew following God "fully" was the key to overcoming and accomplishing the dream.

Completely selling out to God and His cause results in dream fulfillment.

Caleb and his reward of Hebron is also proof for us that *no giant is big enough to keep us from our God-given dreams.* No matter how big, how well fortified, or how long they've been there, God is bigger still. All giants are to be measured against Him.

When it comes to the rules of dreaming and giant-killing, perspective is everything.

One day a father and his rich family took his young son on a trip to the country with the firm purpose of showing him how poor people can be. They spent a day and a night on the farm of a very poor family. When they got back from their trip the father asked his son, "How was the trip?"

"Very good, Dad!"

"Did you see how poor people can be?" the father asked.

"Yeah!"

"And what did you learn?"

The son answered, "I saw that we have a dog at home, and they have four. We have a pool that reaches to the middle of the garden, they have a creek that has no end. We have imported lamps in the garden, they have stars. Our patio reaches to the front yard, they have a whole horizon." When the little boy was finishing, his father was speechless. His son added, "Thanks, Dad, for showing me how poor we are!"[3]

For most of Israel, Arba was just too powerful to overthrow. Caleb had a different perspective. He was just glad the giant had done most of the work of building his city for him, the place where he and God would hang out together.

One more thing can be seen through Hebron. Most people aren't aware that years later King David, another dreamer and friend of God, began his reign in Hebron. Though he eventually ruled Israel from Jerusalem, Hebron saw the birth of his kingdom. Not only do dreams come true at Hebron, "the place of friendship with God," but *authority from Him begins there also.*

The Lord gives authority to those He can trust, and trust is born of relationship. I must admit that my journey with the Lord began with more of a selfish, what's-in-it-for-me outlook. I'm afraid that even some of my early ministry dreams, though I didn't realize it then, were tainted with human ambition and laced with the poison of pride. It is not always easy to recognize the subtle defilements of our soul, especially when our heart is driven by love for God and a desire to serve Him. David knew this and came to the point where he said, "You'll have to search my heart, Lord, to see what's really in there" (see Psalm 139:23–24).

What I can also testify, however, is that just like Abraham, I've grown in my relationship with my heavenly Father. And more than anything else, I want to be His companion, walking and dreaming with Him as His friend. Like Caleb, I'm trying to follow Him fully—I'd like to think He can trust me. When His eyes run to and fro throughout the earth, looking for someone whose heart is completely His (see 2 Chronicles 16:9), I hope they always pause over me.

How about you?

For Review

1. Describe some differences between the two men of faith, Joshua and Caleb, and the other ten spies who searched the Promised Land.

2. What is the significance of Hebron's previous name?

3. Which of the lessons learned from Caleb speaks the most to you at this time of your life? What can you do to apply this personally?

4. What does following God "fully" mean to you?

5. What is the biggest giant in your life with the potential of keeping you from experiencing your destiny? Ask God and, if necessary, others to help you develop a plan to overcome it.

6. What is the connection between Hebron and authority?

14

The Test of Delay

Write the dream. Put it on paper and make sure it's very clear so others who read about it can participate. Remember, the dream is not just for you, it's also for others in the future; at just the right time it will come to pass. You'll see. So even though you're going to have to wait a while, don't give up. The dream will surely happen.

my paraphrase of Habakkuk 2:2–3

Though written by the prophet Habakkuk at a later time in history, this could easily have been written for Abraham. He had reached the friendship state in his relationship with Yahweh, but the strength of that friendship would continue to be tested. And nothing would test it more than God's promise to him of a son. This was Abraham's ultimate dream, for it was the part that gave all of his dreams permanence.

Abraham could not have known the degree to which his and God's dreams were intertwined. There was the veiled statement, of course, "And I will bless those who bless you, and the one who curses you

I will curse and *in you all the families of the earth will be blessed"* (Genesis 12:3). But there was really no way Abraham could have known that the Savior of the world and of God's dream would ultimately come through his offspring.

It was true, however. Their dreams were inseparably intertwined. Perhaps this was why the dream of having a son was going to take a while. Quite a while. No one knows for certain why the Lord waited twenty-five years to give Isaac to Abraham and Sarah. Maybe it was to coincide with the birth of Rebekah, Isaac's eventual wife; perhaps it was simply the exact time in history's progress that he had to be born; or maybe the wait was just to work some character into Abraham and Sarah. We can't be certain. What we do know is that it was a brutal test for both of them.

> **Dreams flowing from God to us will always be intended to bless and benefit others, not just ourselves.**

We also know the birth of Isaac wasn't just for Abraham and Sarah. That's one of the challenges of dreaming, at least when God is involved. He doesn't play solitaire. Now that I've offended your sensibilities by using a card game to reference God's ways, at least hear my point. He isn't into individualism—"a social or ethical doctrine stressing the importance of the individual rather than that of the group; self-assertion in disregard of other." He is into individuality—"the quality or characteristics that make one person different from others"—and made each of us with our own unique personality and giftedness. But when it comes to dreaming, He desires corporality, not individualism. That isn't to say the dream itself must be shared by others, just that when God gives a dream it typically won't be to bless only the person it is given to. He's a giver by nature and wants us to share that nature. The dreams flowing from Him to us will always be intended to bless and benefit others, not just ourselves.

Years ago, a man who changed the eating habits of Americans made sure his influence went beyond the breakfast table. Henry Parsons Crowell was the founder of the Quaker Oats Company. His shrewd business sense and marketing genius brought him to the highest levels in business. His dreaming, however, brought him to the highest levels of Kingdom fruitfulness.

Mr. Crowell was regarded as one of the most respected Christian businessmen in the early twentieth century in the United States. He helped to create entirely new methods of marketing and merchandising that are still revolutionary, even by today's standards. As one of the wealthiest men of Chicago when he died in 1944, he gave away nearly 70 percent of his earnings for more than forty years. He chose to work hard, never compromising, even when doing so would bring him more prosperity.

Crowell viewed all things as a stewardship from God. In whatever he did Crowell sought to honor God, whether it was through business or his forty years as chairman of the board of Moody Bible Institute. Businessmen over the years came to know Jesus Christ personally because of his influence.

The Henry Parsons Crowell and Susan Coleman Crowell Trust carefully states that its purpose is to fund the teaching and active extension of the doctrines of evangelical Christianity. Today, more than seventy-five years later, that directive still guides the Trustees as they disperse funds from the Trust to organizations whose missions are in line with Mr. Crowell's vision. His vision and mission have blessed hundreds of ministries every year all around the world.[1]

It is always inspirational to me when I hear of wealth generators who invest most of their money in Kingdom dreams. They understand that the dream isn't just for them. And such was the case with Abraham. The promise of Isaac was not just for him but for all of us. Therefore, Isaac had to arrive God's way, at God's time. He would, in fact, become a type or shadow (biblical terms meaning something existing now is being used to picture a future reality) of

God's own Son. So Abraham and Sarah would wait, and the dream would be tested.

Both of these dreamers passed the test, though they had to retake portions of it. The privilege of retaking failed tests is one of the benefits of God's grace. He'll allow us to retake them until we pass. His grading system is pass or fail, and though He won't allow us to cheat or opt out, we can retake the exams until we pass.

An example of this with Abraham and Sarah had to do with their faith, which wavered on occasion. When they were well advanced in years, both of them actually laughed in God's face as He restated the promise. Isaac's name actually means "laughter," a mandate from the Lord as a result of this episode. (You can't say the Lord doesn't have a sense of humor.) But in the end they believed. Isaac was born and the laughter of derision became the laughter of joy. Isaac, well, I guess he was stuck with the play on words as his permanent "handle."

There was also a dark season before Isaac came when Abraham lied to a king about Sarah. It seems she was quite beautiful, and Abraham was afraid the king would kill him and take her as his wife. So much for chivalry. But God never said they were perfect. When all was said and done, what mattered most to Him is that they had grown into faithful friends. Dreaming friends.

Like Abraham and Sarah, your dreams, too, will be tested. No one said dreaming was easy. The dream-stealer will try to rob you of your dreams, other individuals will as well, and life itself will throw some curves your way. But don't stop dreaming. Remember, you're not dreaming just for yourself. Others are also depending on them.

Another well-known Abraham, Abraham Lincoln, didn't give up on his dream and was ever persistent. He was born into poverty and faced defeat throughout his life. He lost eight elections and failed in business twice. He tried to get into law school but couldn't. He was once engaged to be married but his sweetheart died. He borrowed money from a friend to start a business and then went bankrupt. He even suffered a total nervous breakdown. Abe ran for congressional office seven times but only won twice. Two years after a defeat in running for the U.S. Senate, he was elected president of the United States (1860). Sometimes the only difference between those who attain and those who don't is perseverance. The great preacher Charles Spurgeon once said, "Through perseverance the snail reached the ark."

Honest Abe didn't quit dreaming, and neither should you. I'm glad he dreamed on. So is our nation—there's a monument in Washington, DC, to his dreaming. And I'm glad our spiritual father, Abraham, kept dreaming, as well; for as it turned out, he was dreaming for all of us. He and Sarah passed the test of delay, and Isaac and his offspring were our reward.

Abraham's dreams were yet to face one more test. This one would push to the brink the limits of his faith in and friendship with God. It turned out to be much more than a test, however. Hidden within it was a look ahead in time and a glimpse into the heart of God, who, as we shall see, became the dreaming champion of the world.

For Review

1. What is the difference between individualism and individuality?

2. How does God use our individuality in the dreaming process?

3. Why are there delays in seeing dreams come to fruition?

4. How do you personally handle the test of delay?

5. Have you had to retake any tests in order to pass them? Why?

6. Think of the person you know who has demonstrated to you the most perseverance. What can you learn from them? Send them a note or call them and thank them. Develop a plan to instill this trait more strongly in yourself.

15

The Dress Rehearsal

By the time we get to the fourth altar in Abraham's life, his dream is alive and doing very well. God has given him land, livestock, servants, great wealth, and, most importantly, Isaac, through whom the promise of becoming a great nation would occur. The Lord and Abraham had walked together for many years and were close friends. But the strength of their relationship would be challenged one more time. The test would be a huge one and would become the pinnacle of their relationship, proving once and for all Abraham's amazing confidence in and loyalty to God.

This event proved to be far more than just a test, however. Hidden in it was one of the most amazing pictures of the cross the Lord ever painted. As we shall see, it demonstrated more than Abraham's trust in God; it was also a heartwarming picture of Jehovah's trust in Abraham.

In Genesis 22, the Lord made a shocking request of Abraham.

"Take now your son, your only son, whom you love, Isaac, and go to the land of Moriah; and offer him there as a burnt offering on one of the mountains of which I will tell you."

Genesis 22:2

Amazing! Ridiculous! Unbelievable! But He said it: *Give me the dream, Abraham. Take that part of the dream which is the most precious to you and sacrifice it to Me.* That would cause just a little bit of a hiccup in your morning devotions.

Abraham must have felt like someone slugged him in the gut. One can only imagine the thoughts and questions that began to swirl through his mind:

- Do I *really* know God's voice as well as I believe I do?
- Do I truly know *Him* as well as I think I do? I don't believe He will make me go through with the sacrifice of Isaac. If He does, I'm convinced He will raise him from the dead.
- With either scenario, what will Isaac think regarding my love for him? Could this so traumatize him that it wounds his psyche, maybe even permanently?

It's impossible to know Abraham's thoughts, but we know he was a good father and loved Isaac very much. We also know there could be no greater test than this of anyone's faith and trust. To say that Abraham passed the test would be the understatement of the millennium. He said yes to questions one and two, and trusted his Friend with number three.

The example this challenges us to emulate in our dreaming seems ridiculously small in comparison to what Abraham had to do. Nonetheless, it is a valid principle that we must always remember: *When God asks for the dream, give it back to Him.* Dreams are powerful. It is possible to so attach our emotions to them that a dream can become a taskmaster we serve, rather than an assignment or goal we steward.

This is precisely what occurred with Adam and Eve, and all of us inherited the virus. Stewarding the dream wasn't enough for them; they became convinced they could own it. At that point, rather than God remaining Lord of the dream, the dream became lord.

Legitimate desires became cravings, even obsessions. We humans have been serving our dreams ever since. We kill for them, abandon family and friends to accomplish and keep them, and spend everything we own to buy them. Since the fall of humanity, God's challenge has been keeping the dream a servant and a tool, rather than allowing it to become the master. Whether the dream is a person, money, possessions, position, or status, the only hope for its purity is keeping it tethered to Him.

A dream can become a taskmaster we serve, rather than an assignment or goal we steward.

It was, of course, never God's intent to allow Abraham to go through with the sacrifice of Isaac. The only human offering He has ever sanctioned was that of Christ on the cross. But at the time Abraham couldn't be certain. He *was* certain, however, of his complete trust in God's character and friendship. Yahweh would either provide a viable substitute for Isaac (see Genesis 22:8), or if He did require him to go through with the sacrifice, the Author and Giver of life would not leave Isaac dead—He would resurrect him (see Genesis 22:5 and Hebrews 11:17–19). What a genuine trust this demonstrated!

Abraham actually saw his obedience as an act of worship. When addressing his servants he said, "I and the lad will go over there; and we will worship and return to you" (Genesis 22:5). This is almost mind-boggling. How many of us could consider a test of this magnitude as worship? When we worship God, we do so because of who He is. He is holy, true, trustworthy, and faithful. Abraham was proving beyond any doubt that He knew God. He was confident the Lord was the Dream-*giver*, not the dream-*stealer*. *I'm not yet sure what this is all about,* Abraham must have reasoned, *but God has something very important He is up to and it's not the death of Isaac.*

Did He ever!

The Dream-giver was Himself dreaming at Moriah. The path to the recovery of His dream would be painful and ugly, and He was about to give us a sneak preview. This entire episode was designed to paint a picture of the cross, where God would one day recapture His dream. No one else knew His plan, not even the angels, but here on this very mountain He would sacrifice His Son and redemption's song would one day be sung.

He was well aware that the violence of this future day would be dreadful beyond description. Creation itself would hide its eyes (see Matthew 27:45) and the very foundations of the earth would shake (see Matthew 27:57). God's heart would break, the angels would watch in shock and horror, and the Son of God Himself would cry out in anguish (see Matthew 27:46). But this violent death would also be love's crowning act.

When the day actually occurred, Satan thought it could become the day of his ultimate victory. This could end God's dream once and for all. Satan did not know the details of God's redemptive plan, but he did know it was somehow wrapped up in His Son. *Kill Him*, he thought. *He has become human, breakable, mortal. Kill Him and kill the dream!* What Satan didn't know—no one but God knew it—was that the cross was part of the dream.

Impossible!

Insane, Satan must have thought.

Actually, it was brilliant. Painfully and devastatingly brilliant, yes, but brilliant nonetheless. And suddenly it all made sense. What looked like one dying Dreamer on a cross was really a dream-seed. There were millions of dreams locked up in Him, waiting to be released. Until the resurrection and Pentecost, Christ's words in John 12:24 were still not understood: "Truly, truly I say to you, unless a grain of wheat falls into the earth and dies, it remains alone; but if it dies, it bears much fruit." He was the grain of wheat, we are the fruit.

That the events on Moriah in Abraham's day were a foreshadowing of Calvary can be seen by several things:

- First, Isaac was referred to as Abraham's "only" or "only begotten son" no less than four times (see Genesis 22:2, 12, 16; Hebrews 11:17), descriptions that were no doubt meant to be prophetic of God's later references to His "only begotten Son" (John 3:16).

- Moriah, the mountain on which Abraham was told to offer Isaac, was the very mountain where centuries later Christ would be offered as our sacrifice. How woefully fitting and strikingly prophetic that Isaac actually carried the wood for the sacrifice up the mountain (Genesis 22:6), just as Christ would one day carry His cross! What must have gone through the Son of God's mind as He watched this unfold!

- Perhaps the most telling proof of all was the name Abraham gave the place when the episode was finished. Predictably, the Lord didn't allow him to go through with the sacrifice. At just the right moment, Abraham saw a substitute ram God had provided, caught in a thicket. After sacrificing the ram, "Abraham called the name of that place The Lord Will Provide [Jehovah Jireh], as it is said to this day, 'In the mount of the Lord it will be provided'" (Genesis 22:14). Though I am fairly certain Abraham didn't know he was prophesying the place of the cross, history confirms that he was.

The poignancy of this dress rehearsal is impossible to overstate. Here was the Creator painting a picture, veiled to all but Himself, of His most cherished dream and horrible nightmare: recapturing His lost family through the death of His Son. *And He is literally doing so on the stage where it will ultimately occur!* Perhaps it was because of the pain of the plan that God wanted one of His best friends to be there with Him.

The name of the mountain where this occurred was also very significant. Moriah actually means "seen of God." Jehovah had taken Abraham there to show him, though in a veiled form, what He was "seeing" in the future—the cross and death of His Son. God must have been deeply impacted as He envisioned the pain, agony, and yet ultimate joy of what would one day take place there. He was also moved by Abraham's complete faith in Him, so much so that He reiterated to him His promise of forty years earlier. The Lord reminded Abraham of *his* dream, also.

> "By Myself I have sworn, declares the Lord, because you have done this thing and have not withheld your son, your only son, indeed I will greatly bless you, and I will greatly multiply your seed as the stars of the heavens and as the sand which is on the seashore; and your seed shall possess the gate of their enemies. In your seed all the nations of the earth shall be blessed, because you have obeyed My voice."
>
> Genesis 22:16–18

God's intentions seem fairly obvious. At this dreaming place, where He would eventually recapture His dream, the Lord wanted Abraham to dream also. Two dreaming friends on a mountain, looking into the future and dreaming together. Incredible. Moving. Wonderful. The following paraphrase sums up the drama of this day:

Remember My promise to you, Abraham. Go ahead, dream.

Here at Moriah, the place where I am seeing My dream, I want you to see yours, as well. Gaze at the stars, envision the sand and see pictures of how I'm going to multiply you.

And though you don't yet realize it, Abraham, My dream is hidden in yours—in your seed all the nations of the earth shall be blessed. Our dreams are completely intertwined, Abraham. Actually, your dream is really all about My dream.

You see stars, I see sons and daughters. You see sand, I see a bride for My Son. You see an altar, I see a cross. You see a ram, I see My Son.

I will bring Him here one day and I'll build an altar in the shape of a cross. . . . I won't stay the knife, but I'll have My dream!

A day for the ages.
A day for friends.

And a day for dreamers everywhere.

An incredibly close friendship must have been necessary for God to become this intimate with Abraham. Taking him to the place where His ultimate dream and ultimate pain would occur demonstrated their closeness. They watched the dress rehearsal together, and years later the consummation did, indeed, take place.

I'm sure these two friends were together again on that day, watching the events unfold and sharing the pain as Isaac's counterpart lay on the "altar." But the pain, excruciating as it was, was temporary. They knew it would be. The dirge did give way to redemption's song—death lost, life won. Then, three days later "Isaac" arose, proving once and for all that the dream was alive and well.

And, I can't prove it, but I think the heavenly choir broke out into Handel's *Messiah*!

For Review

1. Describe the test that occurred prior to Abraham building the fourth altar.

2. What is the significance of the location for this test?

3. What principle was the basis of this test? Why is it important to follow this principle?

4. Explain how God's dream was revealed in this test. Be specific.

5. Because of Abraham's complete faith in Him, what did God then do?

16

The Heel-Grabber

Though Abraham's experience at Moriah pictured the cross where God would recapture His dream of family and redeem us from our fallen nature, the actual fulfillment of the event was still hundreds of years away. Thankfully, at times He was able to find individuals such as Abraham who rose above the self-centeredness of the fall and dreamed with Him. For the most part, however, because we were cut off from our Maker, we had become a race of independent, selfish, earthbound dreamers. With our nature now defiled, selfless dreaming took a backseat to a what's-in-it-for-me mentality, as is pictured by the following account:

> The Los Angeles Lakers . . . began their 1980–1981 season considered likely to win back-to-back championships. But within weeks of the season opener, Magic Johnson tore the cartilage in his knee, and needed a three-month recuperation period.
>
> The team and fans rallied . . . and they were determined to make it through. . . . They were winning seventy percent of their games. . . .
>
> As [Magic's] return grew closer, the publicity surrounding him increased. . . . All the media attention was focused on the one player

who hadn't been doing a thing. Finally [February] 27th came, and as they clicked through the turnstiles every one of the 17,500 ticket holders was handed a button that said, "The Magic Is Back!"

. . . Normally only the starters were introduced, and Magic was going to be on the bench when the game began. But he was nevertheless included in the introductions. At the mention of his name, the arena rocked with a standing ovation. . . .

The other players . . . were so resentful that they barely won the game that night. . . . The morale of the entire team collapsed. The players turned on each other. The coach was fired. And they eventually lost their opening series of the play-offs, having one of the most disastrous records ever.

"Because of greed, pettiness, and resentment," [Coach Pat] Riley later said, "we executed one of the fastest falls from grace in NBA history. It was the Disease of Me."[1]

The Lakers' fall from grace may have been sudden, but the all-time fastest in history occurred in the garden of Eden. The "disease of me" started at the fall. The results were ugly. Genesis 6:5 describes this condition: "Then the Lord saw that the wickedness of man was great on the earth, and that every *intent* of the thoughts of his heart was only evil continually."

"Intent" is the word *yetser,* a term we looked at earlier, which means "thoughts, imaginations, or conceptions" (and obviously would include our dreams). As you may remember, this word comes from the same root as *yatsar,* the Old Testament word for creating. To review, first we *yetser*—imagine or dream; then we *yatsar*—create. This verse says man dreamed of evil continually. Predictably, the "evil" actions mentioned in this verse followed.

The next verse says God "was grieved in His heart." The condition of His longed-for family had broken the Creator's heart. As we have seen, He chose not to give up, however, and promised to bring forth a Savior through Abraham's descendents. One of those family members, who would be a key player in the plan, was going to be a real piece of work before he could become God's partner. In fact, he reminds me of Jason.

You remember Jason. I began the book by talking about him and his grandfather, Red Stevens, from the movie *The Ultimate Gift*. Jason was the guy who had to go through a series of tests and character overhauls before he was qualified for his inheritance.

It seems that Abraham had a grandson like Jason; we know him as Jacob. The similarities in the two stories are interesting, if not remarkable. Both involved family patriarchs, good men who had made a *lot* of money; each had a grandson destined to carry on the family name and dreams but who was initially unfit for the job; both grandsons had "me disease," caring only for themselves and their own dreams; and generally speaking, both had character flaws big enough to turn any blessing into a curse. In short, both young men were unmistakably and pathetically human.

> The "disease of me" started at the fall.

It was while watching this movie in my "Moriah cabin," also mentioned in the Introduction, that God began speaking to me about Jacob. As He walked me back through the years of my life, I saw plenty of Jacob in my actions and dreams. All of us, if we're honest, will admit to Jacob and Jason qualities in our own hearts. And no one, at least as far as God and Red are concerned, should get the dreamed-of inheritance without some serious transformation. Even those of us who think we've dealt with our own Jacob nature by taking it to the cross—the place of its intended execution—are once in a while slapped in the face with the reality that we must take this part of our nature there "daily" (Luke 9:23). It tries to resurrect itself every morning.

No person could picture the post-fall condition of humankind better than Jacob. Dreamer extraordinaire, he fine-tuned the art of post-fall dreaming to a very *low* level. Actually, he got a head start on most of us—he was demonstrating his true nature at birth! As his elder twin, Esau, was being born, Jacob was clutching his heel (see Genesis 25:26). Thus the name Jacob, which means "heel-grabber." Not very imaginative, but it works.

The term is actually much more revealing than a cursory glance might reveal. The root word has a figurative meaning of "circumventing (as if tripping by the heels); also to restrain (as if holding by the heel)." The Brown, Driver, and Briggs Hebrew-English Lexicon, one of the most respected Old Testament reference tools, actually says the word means "assail hideously" or "attack." It goes on to say that a good translation of Genesis 25:26 would be "he attacked his brother at the heel."

So much for brotherly love.

The Amplified Bible picks up on the various nuances of Jacob's name, using the phrase "supplanter, schemer, trickster, swindler" to translate it (see Genesis 32:27). Suffice it to say, the root word often had a negative connotation and proved to be amazingly prophetic for this man. (For all of you actually named Jacob, take heart. Jacob eventually overcame this nature and his name ultimately became associated with honor and greatness.)

True to form, Jacob again demonstrated his conniving heart several years later when he conceived a plan to finagle his elder brother Esau's birthright. The birthright, which belonged to the eldest son, meant that the largest portion of the inheritance would be his. Though Scripture doesn't excuse Esau for selling his birthright for a bowl of soup—his "despising" of it is spoken of as shameful (see Genesis 25:34 and Romans 9:13)—the problem was that Jacob resorted to his supplanting, conniving nature to get it.

A short while later, this same covetous nature manifested yet again when Jacob and his mother hatched a devious plan to steal Esau's final blessing from his father. Jacob was nothing if not consistent! Isaac, old and dying, was making plans to pronounce the traditional parting blessing on his children; Esau's blessing, as the oldest son, would be the greatest.

The heel-grabber had other plans.

All the details aren't necessary, only the fact that the scheme involved a complete deception of his now blind father, Isaac, and a devious manifestation of the Jacob nature (see Genesis 27 for the entire story). You can be fairly confident your dreaming nature has hit an all-time low when you swindle your brother out of his inheritance and deceive your blind, dying father to do so. God was gonna have a lot of work to do on this unrefined dreamer! (Kinda like my editors with my unrefined English. They take out most of my slang verbiage, but once in a while I talk them into leaving a "gonna" or "kinda.")

> **Let's just say God has a lot of faith in His transformational skills.**

Jacob, as it turns out, was God's choice to carry on the family dream and father the messianic race. At this point, however, he was anything but qualified. Far from being God's trustworthy friend, Jacob hadn't yet even chosen the Lord as his God! (See Genesis 28:20–21.) Trusting Jacob as a saving-the-world partner? Well, let's just say God has a lot of faith in His transformational skills. And as Red Stevens with Jason, God knew the treasure that lay buried under the Adamic soil of Jacob's heart.

One of the interesting uses of the Hebrew word from which the name Jacob is derived hints at God's transformational ability. "Every valley shall be exalted, and every mountain and hill shall be made low: and the *crooked* shall be made straight, and the rough places plain" (Isaiah 40:4 KJV). The word *crooked* comes from the same root as the name Jacob. The context of this verse is a prophecy foretelling the ministry of John the Baptist, whose powerful, confrontational, and convicting message of repentance and change prepared the way for Christ's ministry. Through John, the "Jacob" ways were removed, creating a highway on which the Lord could enter.

The Lord was well aware of the "crooked" places in Jacob's heart when He chose him. But He also saw the good in Jacob and knew

He could transform him from a crooked heel-grabber to a world-changing friend. He has similar plans for all of us. Through all the muck and mire of our hearts, He sees a potential dreaming partner. His grace truly is amazing, as slave trader John Newton, an eighteenth-century "Jacob," discovered. If God could "de-Jacob" Newton and make his crooked places straight, there's hope for all of us.

During most of his life, the English-born John Newton was not unlike Jacob. Even though at a young age he attended English schools that prepared students for the ministry, by age ten he was sailing on his first voyage with his father, a strict sea captain. Later, young Newton sailed voyages with a Spanish merchant ship, England's Royal Navy, and then on a slave ship. Because of seeming to get himself in trouble often, Newton was discharged along the African coast, where he went to work for a slave trader. According to biographers, "The trader's wife disliked the young Newton intensely and in an ironic twist of fate convinced the trader that the boy should be treated as a slave. So there he worked, along with the black slaves—poorly fed, poorly clothed, unpaid—for about a year. Newton was finally rescued by another white slave trader and later returned to England on the ship *Greyhound*.

It was on the *Greyhound* that John turned back to his Christian roots. But his refound religion didn't alter his views on slavery. Five years later, as captain of his own ship, he wrote in his journal that he was thankful for being led into "an easy and creditable way of life." Newton was not alone in this despicable way of thinking. In 1753 when he wrote the entry, the slave trade was respectable and, in England, overwhelmingly accepted.

After four years as a slave ship captain, Newton resigned his commission on the advice of his doctors. By this time his views on the trade had begun to change. Several years later, after becoming a minister, he wrote, "I think I should have quitted [the slave trade] sooner had I considered it as I now do to be unlawful and wrong. But I never had a scruple upon this head at the time; nor was such a thought ever suggested to me by any friend."

Newton would eventually be a significant voice for the abolition of the slave trade. In 1797, we are told, he stated,

> If the trade is at present carried on to the same extent and nearly in the same manner, while we are delaying from year to year to put a stop to our part in it, the blood of many thousands of our helpless, much injured fellow creatures is crying against us. The pitiable state of the survivors who are torn from their relatives, connections, and their native land must be taken into account.

Newton realized what the slavery industry had made him. And after receiving Christ and becoming an advocate for its eradication, he penned these famous words:

> Amazing grace, how sweet the sound
> That saved a wretch like me.
> I once was lost, but now am found,
> Was blind, but now I see.

Just before Newton's death in 1807, the English government officially brought to a close its participation in the slave trade.[2]

Thank God for His amazing grace—and the song. Some historians actually believe Newton took the melody for "Amazing Grace" from the singing of slaves aboard one of his ships. Whether or not this is the case, I'm sure it originated in heaven, and we are all grateful the Lord was persistent in dealing with the Jacob nature of John Newton. He transformed his dream of wealth gained at the expense of others into a dream of serving and liberating his fellowman. Newton's song, "Amazing Grace," has been sung more than any other song in history. Often sung at funerals, it has become one of the all-time great "dirge to dream" songs.

As I pondered Jacob's journey in my cabin retreat a few years back, and watched *The Ultimate Gift* movie yet again, I couldn't help but think how gracious and patient God is with us. And relentless. I knew He had been with me.

I thought about my past, faced the reality that it was now longer than my future, and determined to make the latter years count for something more than "Jacob dreams." *More than anything,* I thought, *I want to spend my remaining years living at Hebron, the place representing friendship with God.*

Jacob, as we shall see, made it to that special place. If he could, so can we.

For Review

1. Describe Jacob's nature. How did his name picture this?

2. Describe the three instances given which revealed Jacob's supplanting nature.

3. Comment on Genesis 6:5–6—what it demonstrates about the fall and also what it shows about God's heart.

4. God knows the fallen Adamic nature we are born with, and yet still sees our potential as dreamers. Evaluate how much of this nature has been conquered by the cross (see Luke 9:23). Make a plan to consistently take other parts of your nature there.

5. Think about John Newton and his radical transformation. What are the limits on God's ability to change and redeem a life? Allow it to build faith in you for yourself and those you love.

17

Jacob's Dreams

Jacob's life took a decided turn after he swindled Esau out of his blessing. Esau had had enough of Jacob's heel-grabbing ways: "Is he not rightly named Jacob, for he has supplanted me these two times? He took away my birthright, and behold, now he has taken away my blessing" (Genesis 27:36).

Not any higher on the honor scale, Esau decided he would kill Jacob (see Genesis 27:41). There was only one recourse for Jacob—he would need to leave for a while. He and Mom decided he should visit his uncle Laban until Esau cooled off, then return home. It shouldn't take too long.

Or so they thought.

God had other plans for Jacob. As his grandfather Abraham had done, he was about to begin a dream journey. Jacob's, however, would be different—God has to tailor-make all dream journeys—but it would end at the same destination: friendship with God. The Lord had to dig a little deeper to find gold in Jacob, but it was there. He began the process by sovereignly leading Jacob to Bethel, "the house of God," on his flight to Laban's. Approximately one hundred years had passed since God met with Abraham there, so it was no longer a place celebrated or even recognized by Jacob. It certainly was to God, however.

When Jacob arrived at Bethel, most translations simply say he arrived at "a" place. What the Hebrew text actually says, however, is he came to "the" place (Genesis 28:11). This was a special location to God—He had begun His dream recovery project here with Abraham, and here He would continue it.

That night as Jacob slept, the Lord gave him an astonishing dream:

> He had a dream, and behold, a ladder was set on the earth with its top reaching to heaven; and behold, the angels of God were ascending and descending on it. And behold, the Lord stood above it and said, "I am the Lord, the God of your father Abraham and the God of Isaac; the land on which you lie, I will give it to you and to your descendants. Your descendants will also be like the dust of the earth, and you will spread out to the west and to the east and to the north and to the south; and in you and in your descendants shall all the families of the earth be blessed. Behold, I am with you and will keep you wherever you go, and will bring you back to this land; for I will not leave you until I have done what I have promised you."
>
> Genesis 28:12–15

With even a casual comparison of these words to those made to Jacob's grandfather Abraham in Genesis 12, the similarities are obvious. The land, material blessings, protection, and many descendents—it's all there, including the part about all the families of the earth being blessed through him. It was a dream for Jacob, with God's dream tucked neatly inside.

The Lord had just deposited His most valuable dream in the hands of a conniving, swindling heel-grabber! When it comes to the risk-taking qualification for dreaming, God sets the standard.

With a visitation like this, I'm sure Jacob felt pretty special. He was nothing if not convinced of his value. He actually *was* special and chosen, but his calling was connected to his grandfather Abraham, not because of his own inherent greatness. The dream God was giving him was simply a continuation of Abraham's. Bethel was one of the places where He began the dream journey with Abraham, and this is unquestionably why the Lord chose to reveal it to Jacob there.

Most of our dreaming is done on the shoulders of someone who went before us. Bethel teaches us that this is not only okay, it is God's plan. Whether it is the dream itself, our inherited gifts and abilities, or the training we've received, someone before us contributed to our dream.

Abraham had met with God at Bethel and built an altar there, making it a holy place with an open heaven. Where he knelt, a future generation could dream God-dreams—his altar sanctified the ground, making it a bed on which Jacob dreamed. One generation's dream and altar becomes the bridge upon which the following generation crosses into its dreams. It is significant that when Jacob's God-encounter ended, he, like Abraham, built an altar at Bethel (see 28:18). *We haven't dreamed successfully until the next generation embraces the dream and builds an altar next to ours.*

In Al Sanders's book, *Crisis in Morality!*, he compares descendants of an atheist named Max Jukes to the offspring of a well-known preacher that lived during Mr. Jukes' lifetime, Jonathan Edwards:

> Max Jukes . . . married an ungodly girl and among their descendants were 310 who died as paupers, 150 as criminals, 7 as murderers, 100 as drunkards and more than half of the women were prostitutes.
>
> But, praise the Lord, it works both ways! Jonathan Edwards . . . lived at the same time but married a godly girl. An investigation was made of 1,394 known descendants of Jonathan Edwards. Of these descendants, 13 became college presidents, 65 college professors, 3 United States senators, 30 judges, 100 lawyers, 60 physicians, 75 army and navy officers, 100 preachers and missionaries, 60 authors

of prominence, one a vice-president of the United States, 80 became public officials . . . and 295 college graduates, among whom were governors of states and ministers to foreign countries.[1]

Could any illustration be more convincing that our lives and dreams prepare the way for the generations following us? The fruit of Edwards's life and dream laid a foundation for those to come. Like Abraham, he dreamed with God and the dream multiplied. Don't dream only for today. Instill into your children and grandchildren the heart of a godly dreamer, and if you do, you'll still be changing the world a hundred years from now.

> **Don't dream only for today. Instill into your children and grandchildren the heart of a godly dreamer.**

Although Jacob was deeply impacted by Bethel and its visitation, he nevertheless left there with his Jacob-nature fully intact. God would have to deal with that later. For now, Jehovah had accomplished what He intended, planting the seeds of the generational dream.

True to form, Jacob hadn't left Bethel before he "Jacob-ed" the dream, thinking only of what *he* might receive from it. What *God* might want or need from it had faded into the recesses of his conniving mind. *This would be a good time to cut a deal with God,* he reasoned. So he laid out his plan: "If you do these things for me," he basically told the Lord, "then you can be my God. Oh, and by the way," he continued, "if you do all this for me, I'll also tithe to you" (see verses 20–22).

What a deal for God!

The ignorance, arrogance, and audacity of this guy is almost laughable. God, and some of His angels, mind you, has just visited Jacob, offering him a partnership. Rather than seeing it as an opportunity to dream with God, Jacob attempts to advance his own cause. This earth-level dreamer sees "God's house" only through the lens of selfish provision and blessing, not as an invitation to choose God as his Father.

It is interesting that Jacob, unlike Abraham, skipped Shechem where Jehovah is chosen as one's God. The Lord would eventually get Jacob there, but it would take a couple of decades. Twenty years later, after another God-encounter that changed his nature, he went to Shechem, built an altar, and finally called the Lord his God (see Genesis 33:18–20). Years of pain could have been avoided had he found it sooner.

Before we cast the first stone, however, we should remember that for most of us, our trip to the altar and entrance into God's house also began primarily for the benefits we could accrue. As with Jacob, we skip Shechem, wanting provision and blessing for our dreams without first accepting God's terms. The next phases of our journey, where He becomes our Father and Friend, are unreachable until this occurs. Many Christians in our culture today never arrive at these destinations. They travel through life dreaming only for themselves, never even realizing Hebron or Moriah exists. What a loss of destiny!

One of the sad dream stories of our day is Michael Jackson, who squandered one of the biggest fortunes ever made by a singer.

> At one point Michael Jackson was worth close to $1 billion. . . . The financial decline began in 1988 with the £10 million [$14.6 million] acquisition of the 2,600-acre Neverland estate, which has been abandoned since 2005. . . . He continued to live the life of a superstar travelling with a 15-person strong entourage in private jets and staying in hotel suites costing £7,000-a-night. He spent hundreds of thousands of pounds on doctors, dermatologists, and plastic surgeons and indulging his passion for electronic gadgets and Neverland.
>
> In the end everybody who knew Jackson also knew that the world's most successful recording artist was no longer even a millionaire though he lived like a billionaire.[2]

Jackson was in debt for around $400 million when he died.[3] What a loss. With his talent and creativity, Jackson could have impacted the world for Christ by writing and performing songs that promoted morality, family, and friendship with God. But like so many who are blessed with exceptional talent, their dreams leave God out of the picture and their destiny is squandered.

Do not make this mistake. Allow Him into your dream. Though you may not have the wealth of Michael Jackson, an NBA superstar, or a Hollywood actor, you have gifts that are valuable to God. Let Him into your dreaming world. There is no ultimate satisfaction or success apart from Him.

King Solomon, perhaps the richest man that ever lived, who also had one thousand wives and concubines, said at the end of his life, "So I hated life, for the work that had been done under the sun was grievous to me; because everything is futility and striving after wind" (Ecclesiastes 2:17). Solomon discovered too late that only dreaming with God brings permanent and eternal contentment.

Like Michael Jackson or King Solomon, Jacob's life could have ended with the loss of everything and despair over a wasted life . . . that is, had God not interrupted his life with another meeting. The Lord was about to deal with his Jacob-nature and elevate him from the status of a heel-grabber to a heavenly dreamer. As is so often the case with life-changing events, the encounter would be painful yet wonderful.

Let's go to Peniel.

For Review

1. God gave Jacob a dream which was a continuation of Abraham's. Who has contributed to your dream?

2. How are you building a bridge for the next generation to pursue the dream and build an altar next to yours?

3. Describe Jacob's response to the dream God gave him.

4. How does this picture the way most of us enter God's family?

5. Think about your hopes and dreams. Have you allowed God to "own" His portion or have you "Jacob-ed" some or all of them? If so, determine now to give Him His portion of the dream.

18

The Face of God

By the time we get from Bethel to Jacob's return trip home, twenty years have passed. What he thought would be a relatively short hiatus from Esau's wrath has now become two decades. Jacob is still "Jacob," but that is about to change. Though unaware of it, God is coming to deal with his heel-grabbing ways.

Jacob has done well. The Lord has already fulfilled much of what He promised him at Bethel. But not unlike many of us, even after such abundant blessing Jacob is still thinking primarily of himself. He has been more than happy to embrace the blessings of God's house, but what Yahweh might need or want from him is nowhere on Jacob's radar. Like we so often do, *he has "Jacob-ed" God's dream.*

Jacob actually remembers Bethel quite well. On his way home he reiterates the promises of blessing and protection made to him there as he prays for protection from Esau, whom he will soon face. It was impressive how well Jacob remembered God's promises after twenty years.

Not so impressive is how completely he had forgotten the portion containing God's dream: "And in you and in your descendents shall all the families of the earth be blessed" (Genesis 28:14). It isn't even mentioned. Just as the Dream-giver had done with Abraham, He had tucked what He needed from the dream into the promises He made to Jacob. I'm not sure Jacob even heard that significant part. If so, it certainly didn't make much of an impression. He was so focused on earthly dreams, he couldn't see heaven's. Jacob was dreaming big; God wanted him to dream *high*. Earthly dreams gave him wealth; heavenly dreams would give him a place in history.

Undeterred by the rejection, God moves Jacob closer to an encounter with Himself that would forever deliver him of his self-seeking, supplanting nature. The Lord, with His mighty but gracious power, was about to break Jacob; with His mercy He was going to mark him. And when God was finished they would dream together.

On the journey, Jacob moves ever closer to a confrontation with Esau. Esau has heard of his approach and is on his way to meet Jacob with four hundred men. True to form, conniving Jacob devises a plan to appease his still-offended brother, sending a series of gifts ahead. As he continues on his way, he ultimately sends everything and everyone, even his family. It must have been a painful sight as he watched them cross the stream called Jabbok, wondering if he would ever see them again (see Genesis 32:22).

It would be easy to miss the irony and significance of this if you didn't know the meaning of *Jabbok*. It means "pouring out." And if you think this is a coincidence, you're officially a cynic.

What a scene.

Jacob, who has spent his entire life conniving his way around and through every obstacle in his path, is wealthy—very wealthy—and has proven he is at the top of the food chain when it comes to dreaming.

Or so he thought.

God had an appointment with Jacob at Jabbok, and in a day everything was gone, poured out to the brother he had swindled twenty years earlier. Forty years of hard "Jacob-ing" and it was all gone in a day.

Jacobs are no match for God.

The next verse sums up his condition and sets the stage for what is about to occur: "Then Jacob was left alone" (Genesis 32:24). Jacob has bought and connived his way out of trouble and into prosperity for the last time. He isn't yet aware of it, but Esau has become the least of his worries. He is alone with God—and this time it isn't for sweet dreams. As preposterous as it sounds, Jacob and God will spend the night wrestling (see verse 24).

The heavenly adversary begins by dislocating Jacob's thigh. Again, the symbolism is powerful. A person's thigh represents his or her strength. Not only have his possessions and family been "poured out," God has now removed his strength. But there are not many people who could be as stubborn as Jacob. Still he fought.

"I won't let you go until you bless me," he says to his opponent, whom many scholars believe was an Old Testament, preincarnate appearance of Christ Himself. What is this blessing Jacob wants? Protection from Esau, of course.

The Lord's response to this is so bizarre it almost sounds like a verse or two have been omitted. That is, until you see what is really happening. "What is your name?" He asks Jacob (Genesis 32:27). Try to picture this: two men fighting, one limping but holding on for dear life while demanding a blessing, and the other—who obviously knows His opponent—demanding to know his name. What is going on?

The Amplified Bible gives the clearest explanation I've seen or heard for this scenario. It translates Jacob's response in verse 27 this way: "And [in shock of realization, whispering] he said, Jacob [supplanter, schemer, trickster, swindler]!" This was a confession of his true nature.

Finally! At last, Jacob is acknowledging his condition.

True to his nature, Jacob had been seeking yet another blessing; God, however, was pursuing Jacob.

"It isn't your possessions, servants, or family I want, Jacob," God may have told him. "It's your Jacob-nature that I'm trying to pour out of you. You can con everyone else, but you can't con Me. I want you to realize, once and for all, that your 'strength' is not what I need from you. I need for you to acknowledge your weakness and who you really are. Only then can I deliver you from yourself. I could kill you, but I'd rather conquer you. Then we can dream together."

The fight was over the moment Jacob acknowledged his true condition. God's goal wasn't to win a fight but to win a heart. And what did He do next? Demonstrating His matchless grace, He changed this former heel-grabber's name: "Your name shall no longer be Jacob, but Israel" (verse 28). Does that not just make you want to dance!

When God wrestled with Jacob He was warring for His dream!

In a matchless display of His grace, wisdom, and persistent love, God transformed this conniving swindler into a prince and patriarch. His sovereign actions made clear the plan, and in so many ways, God told him: "Now we can get on with the dream, Israel. Because the dream isn't just for you; it's for Me, as well. And for the generations to follow. I need a nation through whom I can demonstrate to the world My ways and heart, and through whom I can bring the Messiah. You're going to birth that nation for Me."

When God wrestled with Jacob, He wasn't fighting only for the heart of a man; He was warring for His dream!

Israel, leaving the fight with a life-altering limp, decided to name the place Peniel, meaning "the face of God," for "I have seen God face to face," he said (Genesis 32:30). Twenty years earlier Jacob entered Bethel, "the house of God," and found a dream. This day he had seen "the face of God" and found the Dream-giver. He would never be the same.

Oh, and what about Esau? God changed his heart, too. He forgave Jacob, now Israel, and gave back the gifts that had been sent ahead. At least he tried to. Jacob would have taken them all back, but Israel, with his new nature, insisted that Esau at least keep some of them!

Let's visit my Moriah cabin once more, only this time I'll call it Peniel, for God and I sparred a little there. *Give Me every dream*, He said, *for yourself, your family, your ministry, and your nation—trust Me with everything.*

Fearfully, oh so humanly, but from a trust born of spending thousands of hours with Him over the years, I reached deep into my heart and pulled out every dream I could find.

He took them, looked at each one, then set them down. Ignoring them, He reached in and began to work on my heart. "It's not the dreams I need, son," He spoke to me. "I just need to get them out of the way temporarily so I can do a little fine-tuning on your heart."

I experienced a broad range of emotions that day as He kneaded and shaped my heart. I laughed a little, thought a lot, and cried once or twice. He was gentle but firm and resolute. He healed, adjusted, fixed a "valve" or two, and unclogged some "blockages." When He was finished I felt both undone and redone.

Then He put the dreams back—well, most of them. Some I didn't need anymore. Those He did put back seemed somehow different. They were still mine but seemed to reflect a little more of His character, heart, and desires. I knew we could now share our lives and dreams at a higher level.

And our friendship had grown.

Like Jacob, I limped home a happy man.

For Review

1. The story in this chapter reveals Jacob demanded a blessing. God intended to bless him, but in a far greater and more

meaningful way than he comprehended. What had to be "poured out" of Jacob before he could receive the blessing?

2. What two things was God fighting for when He wrestled Jacob?

3. What was the significance of God dislocating Jacob's thigh?

4. When Jacob was finally changed, Esau's heart toward him was changed. What can we learn from this?

5. Jacob named the place Peniel. What is the significance of this?

6. Plan a special time with the Lord. Give your dreams back to Him, then allow Him to give back to you those He wants you to keep. Make sure you also find His dream(s) in the process.

Epilogue

There are times in my life when I am simply in awe of the workings of the Lord. Today is one of those days. It has been three years since my life was so deeply impacted by God in my Moriah/ Peniel cabin and He began speaking with me about dreams. Through His providential leading I now find myself back at that very place, putting the finishing touches on the book. Several months ago when Ceci and I planned a few days of vacation, I had no idea the timing would coincide with the finishing of the book—but the Dream-giver did.

God is so amazing!

At the moment, I'm sitting next to the stream, gazing at the altar and cross on the small island, thinking about that day three years ago and the impact it has had on me. As is typical, the revelation has grown through the marinating process of study, meditation, and prayer.

I'm staying in a different cabin, by the way. This seemed a little strange, initially. *If God were going to bring me back here to finish the book*, I wondered, *why wouldn't He make certain the same cabin was available?* Then I saw the plaque:

JOURNEY
"'For I know the plans I have for you,' declares the Lord . . ."
Jeremiah 29:11

This is not a Christian camp, by the way; it is simply a community of privately owned dwellings, some of which can be rented. I wonder if the owner of this one had any idea when she purchased the plaque that it would be used by the Holy Spirit in such a remarkable way?

Have I mentioned yet that God is amazing?!

As this phase of my journey comes to an end, a new one will begin. My dream of writing this book is ending, but as this verse so powerfully states, the Lord has more plans for me, "plans for welfare and not calamity, to give [me] a future and a hope." "Future" is the word *acharyith*, sometimes translated "destiny." I'm confident that my destiny is secure in the dreaming heart of my heavenly Father.

> **When God captures a piece of your heart, always build an altar there!**

I'll bring my children and grandchildren to this cabin one day and we'll discuss the truths the Holy Spirit revealed to me. I'll pray with them and point out the island with the altar and cross as I pass on my dreams, and my dreaming heart, to my children. I could relate it to them from elsewhere, but not as powerfully as I'll be able to in this place.

As I sit here looking at the altar, I'm building one in my heart, just as I did three years ago. When God captures a piece of your heart, always build an altar there!

It is so fascinating to me that after fully capturing Jacob's heart, the Lord told him to go back to Bethel, the place where the dreams began, and live (see Genesis 35:1). "Oh, and build another altar there," the Lord also told him (my paraphrase). Jacob obeyed and named the altar El Bethel, which means "the God of Bethel."

"The God of the dream place"—what a name!

"This is where the journey began," the name was implying. "You gave my grandfather a dream at this place, and You visited me with a dream here, as well. I want You to know, God, that I honor You as the Dream-giver and that from this day forward we will dream together."

By telling Jacob to live at Bethel, the Lord was also making a huge statement. "Since I've captured your heart, Jacob, and can now trust you as My dreaming partner, why don't you just go back there and live. In that special place where it began . . . let's live the dream!"

If that doesn't move you, you're immovable!

Now, friend, it is time for you to dream. As the plaque in my cabin states, the Lord has plans for you. He has Bethel's and Peniel's, Hebron's and Moriah's. His dreaming heart has dreamed about you, and you must find these dreams. Let nothing stop you. You can be confident of His faithfulness to show you the plans He has for you.

Now, I think I'm gonna put pen and paper down, sit here by the stream with my Friend, and dream a little.

Notes

Chapter 1: The Power of Dreams

1. Spiros Zodhiates, ed., *Hebrew-Greek Key Word Study Bible* (Chattanooga: AMG, 1990), 1732.

2. Jack Canfield and Mark Victor Hansen, *Chicken Soup for the Soul* (Deerfield Beach, FL: Health Communications, 1993), 162–163.

Chapter 2: The Dreaming God

1. Gene Edwards, *The Divine Romance* (Carol Stream, IL: Tyndale House, 1984, 1992), 3–4.

2. Jack Canfield, Mark Hansen, Jennifer Hawthorne, and Marci Shimoff, *Chicken Soup for the Mother's Soul* (Deerfield Beach, FL: Health Communications, 1997), 165–166.

Chapter 3: The Song

1. Alice Gray, *More Stories for the Heart* (Sisters, OR: Multnomah, 1997), 220.

Chapter 4: Born to Dream

1. Earl Nightingale, "Sparky—Charlie Brown," in *More Sower's Seeds*, ed. Brian Cavanaugh (Mahwah, NJ: Paulist Press, 1992), 54–55.

2. Adapted from Jack Canfield and Mark Victor Hansen, *Chicken Soup for the Soul* (Deerfield Beach, FL: Health Communications, 1993), 201–202.

3. Craig Brian Larson, *Illustrations for Preaching and Teaching* (Grand Rapids: Baker, 1993), 38.

Chapter 5: Destiny Dreaming

1. Denis Waitley and Reni L. Witt, *The Joy of Working* (New York: Ballantine Books, 1985), 33.

2. Myles Munroe, *Releasing Your Potential* (Shippensburg, PA: Destiny Image, 1992), 10.

3. Steven G. Dyer, *Transforming a Nation* (Grove, OK: Steven G. Dyer, 2010), 54.

Chapter 6: Dream or Decorate

1. Craig Brian Larson, *Illustrations for Preaching and Teaching* (Grand Rapids: Baker, 1993), 280.

2. Zodhiates, *Hebrew-Greek Key Word Study Bible*, 1766.

Chapter 7: Get Motivated

1. Adapted from Jack Canfield and Mark Victor Hansen, *A 2nd Helping of Chicken Soup for the Soul* (Deerfield Beach, FL: Health Communications, 1995), 254–255.

Chapter 8: Hounds and Roosters

1. Craig Brian Larson, *Contemporary Illustrations for Preachers, Teachers, and Writers* (Grand Rapids: Baker, 1996), 183.

Chapter 9: The Dream Mix

1. Kevin Shorter, "Faith the Size of a Peanut," *Prayer Coach* (blog), November 10, 2010, http://shorterdesigns.com/prayercoach/2010/11/10/faith-the-size-of-a-peanut/.

2. Adapted from "Gladys Aylward: 'I Wasn't First Choice for What I've Done in China,'" HistoryMakers, accessed January 11, 2012, http://www.historymakers.info/inspirational -christians/gladys-aylward.html.

3. Adapted from Roger Steer, "Pushing Inward," *Christian History: Hudson Taylor and Missions to China* 15, no. 4 (1996): http://www.christianitytoday.com/ch/1996/issue52/52h10a. html ; and adapted from Ralph R. Covell, "Taylor, James Hudson," *Biographical Dictionary of Chinese Christianity*, ed. Gerald H. Anderson (New York: MacMillan Reference USA, 1998), reprinted online at http://www.bdcconline.net/en/stories/t/taylor-james-hudson.php.

Chapter 10: The Senior Partner

1. "About S. Truett Cathy," S. Truett Cathy website, accessed June 7, 2011, http://www .truettcathy.com/about_bio.asp.

2. Al Bryant, "Job Wasn't Big Enough," *Encyclopedia of 7700 Illustrations*, ed. Paul Lee Tan (Rockville, MD: Assurance, 1979), 815.

3. Craig Brian Larson, *Illustrations for Preaching and Teaching* (Grand Rapids: Baker, 1993), 262.

Chapter 11: Choices

1. Edward K. Rowell, *Fresh Illustrations for Preaching and Teaching* (Grand Rapids: Baker, 1997), 147.

Chapter 12: Dreaming With Friends

1. Craig Brian Larson, *Contemporary Illustrations for Preachers, Teachers, and Writers* (Grand Rapids: Baker, 1996), 187.

Chapter 13: Caleb

1. http://www.innocentenglish.com/movie-quotes-database/movie-quote-database-free/movie-quotes-from-braveheart.html.

2. Craig Brian Larson, *Contemporary Illustrations for Preachers, Teachers, and Writers* (Grand Rapids: Baker, 1996), 47.

3. "Perspectives," *Inspiration Peak*, accessed May 30, 2011, http://www.inspirationpeak.com/cgi-bin/stories.cgi?record=24.

Chapter 14: The Test of Delay

1. Adapted from Joe Musser, *The Cereal Tycoon* (Chicago: Moody Press, 2002), 3, 154, back cover.

Chapter 16: The Heel-Grabber

1. Robert J. Morgan, *Real Stories for The Soul* (Nashville: Thomas Nelson, 2000), 20–22.

2. *Africans in America*, "John Newton," PBS Online, www.pbs.org/wgbh/aia/part1/1p275.html.

Chapter 17: Jacob's Dreams

1. Quoted in Leonard Ravenhill, "Jonathan Edwards: Portrait of a Revival Preacher," *Dayspring*, 1963, www.ravenhill.org/edwards.htm.

2. Andrew Pierce, "Michael Jackson Squandered One of Biggest Fortunes Ever Earned by a Singer," *The Telegraph*, June 26, 2009, http://www.telegraph.co.uk/culture/music/michael-jackson/5652573/Michael-Jackson-squandered-one-of-biggest-fortunes-ever-earned-by-a-singer.html.

3. "Michael Jackson's Death: King of Pop Was Awash in Debt," *Huffington Post*, July 27, 2009, http://www.huffingtonpost.com/2009/06/26/michael-jacksons-death-ki_n_221303.html.

DUTCH SHEETS is an internationally known speaker and author. He has written many books, including the bestseller *Intercessory Prayer*. For eighteen years, Dutch pastored Freedom Congregation in Colorado Springs. He travels extensively throughout the United States empowering believers for passionate prayer and world-changing revival. His greatest passion is to see awakening in our day and reformation in our lifetime. Dutch, Ceci, his wife of over thirty years, and their three dogs reside in Hamilton, Alabama.

Joe,
you were
designed to
dream & you must ...
both for yourself & God.
Always know & remember
that God loves you.
achieve your destiny! June 2013